Luciana Savelli

SICILY
and its Islands

400 color photos · Map of the region

EVERYTHING THERE IS TO KNOW
ABOUT THIS EXTRAORDINARY LAND

BONECHI EDIZIONI "IL TURISMO"

Extraordinary Sicily

*T*his book is in itself a journey through the length and breadth of Sicily, the Sicily of the three promontories: Cape Peloro at Messina, Cape Boeo at Marsala, and Cape Passero, seductive Trinakria *in the midst of the Mediterranean Sea, surrounded by islands, a bridge between Africa and Europe, between the East and the West.*

Many-faceted Sicily: art and history, sea and mountains, volcanic fire and fertile plains, subtle and violent colors and sounds, noble and poor, a land of dreams and of crime, of passions and rationality, of proletarian work and noble indolence, harmonious and ambiguous. It is a land that attracts and repels, but a visit to this land "where orange blossoms bloom" is enriching. All the more so since the island is currently undergoing a renaissance, its vast cultural patrimony protected by the European Institutions, rediscovered by international tourism and with the Sicilians themselves, committed to uprooting the ancient scourge of the Mafia, participating in this renaissance, symbolized by the great project of the bridge over the Strait of Messina.

Sicily is a land where myth and history have merged, where gods and nymphs fell in love but where who prevailed was the goddes. The archetype of femininity, the great Mother Goddess, *who lived here ceded her throne to the Virgin Mary, the mother who incarnates the sufferings of mankind. Few other places can boast of such overwhelming Marian de-* votion and worship and such a multitude of churches and shrines.

For three thousand years Sicily has been the land of arrivals and departures, crossroads and crucible of peoples, races, religions and civilizations. The tangible signs of their passage are in what is essentially a single unrivaled archaeological park, as well as in the many souls of Sicily and of the Sicilians.

Rock graffiti, the burials in the tophet, *the solemn magnificent temples and the elegant Arab traceries, the Arab-Norman stylistic features and the imposing Swabian castles, the scenic flowery Spanish Baroque, and Art Nouveau with its plant motifs, all bear witness to the presence of the native Siculi, the Phoenicians, Greeks and Carthaginians, the Byzantines and the Arabs, Normans and Swabians and Spanish. Thirteen different rules in thirty centuries left blonde hair, blue eyes and white skin, curly heads of hair, flashing dark eyes and olive skin. Work in the sulfur fields and tuna fishing is giving way to tourism and the rediscovery of the marvelous traditional cuisine.*

It was in the Sicily of these golden centuries, discoursing on love, women and arms, that Italian literature began with the Sicilian school of poetry, continuing with authors, poets, thinkers and the Nobel prize in literature in the recent twentieth century.

Goethe, after visiting the island said that Italy would be nothing without Sicily.

▲ The crystal-clear sea of Terrasini.

● Landscape and territory

Located in the middle of the Mediterranean, Sicily is an island separated from Italy by three kilometers of sea, surrounded by the small islands of Ustica and Pantelleria and the Aeolian, Egadi and Pelagian archipelagoes. It is the largest region in Italy with its 25,708 sq. km. and 1500 km of coast, including the islands. Bathed by three seas, the Tyrrhenian, the Ionian and the Mediterranean, it is seventy kilometers from Africa. Beaches of white sand, pulverized shells, or black lava, and reefs dot the coastline, broken up by inlets and scenic gulfs: Milazzo, Patti, Palermo and Castellammare, cities bathed by an extraordinary crystal clear sea, ranging from turquoise green to African blue, with untold archaeological deposits, marine flora and fauna in its abysses. Along the coasts the Sicilian climate is mild, while inland the winters are harsher and snowy. Summers are scorching and arid and the thermometer can climb to forty de-

► The lush forest in the Nebrodi Park.

3

▲ The saltpans in the Nature Reserve of Trapani.

grees C in the shade. But spring comes early in February and summer lasts till October.

The Peloritani, Nebrodi and Madonie mountain chains cut across Sicily, with peaks as high as 2000 meters. The uplands of the Erei mountains – sulfur bearing hills of limestone and chalk, and the Iblei – ridges cut by narrow ravines and deep valleys, eroded by water, are low and arid. With its 3,323 meters Mount Etna "*a muntagna*" is the highest massif and the largest active volcano in Europe. Florid vegetation and cultivated crops cover the fertile lava soil on the slopes of its perennially snow-covered cone. Two islands, Vulcano and Stromboli, are still active volcanoes while the smaller islands of Linosa, Pantelleria and Ustica are only of volcanic origin.

There are few rivers in Sicily and the plains are the Conca d'Oro and the Plain of Catania, the most important with 430 sq. km of cultivations and orange groves, crossed by the Simeto River on its way to the Ionian sea. The Salso with its 144 km is the longest river followed by the Platani with 84, the Belice with 76 and lastly the Sosio 53 km. long. All in all Sicily is a thirsty land, where rain is scarce and never enough. The region tries to keep the "thirst" emergency at bay with artificial basins and desalinating installations.

◄ Etna, the volcano that dominates the plain.

► Sicana necropolis of Caltabellotta.

TOMBE
SICANE

● History

Inhabited in prehistory, the peoples, races and cultures that passed through Sicily in three thousand years of foreign rule have left their mark. The Sesiotes, primitive peoples who extracted obsidian in Pantelleria, were followed by the Siculi, the Sicani and the Elymians, said to be descendents of the mythical Trojans who built the cities of Erice and Segesta.

The Phoenicians on the west coast founded Palermo, Solunto and Mozia, created emporia, textile and dying workshops, trade with the Mediterranean. In the eighth century BC the Greeks colonized eastern Sicily and built their splendid *poleis*: Agrigento, Syracuse, Gela, Catania, centers of culture and trade with their own coinage, marking the beginnings of the civilization we are heirs to.

Greek Sicily at the time rivaled Athens in power and wealth and built magnificent temples to its gods.

The frequent conflicts between Greeks and Phoenicians in Sicily came to an end in 480 BC with the *battle of Himera* when Greek superiority prevailed. Hostilities continued with the Carthaginians who were extending their borders in their attempts to take control of the Mediterranean until their defeat by the Romans in the three *Punic wars*, between 264 and 146 BC.

Sicily became a Roman province. The new conquerors introduced large landed estates and the island became

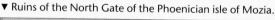

▼ Ruins of the North Gate of the Phoenician isle of Mozia.

the granary of Rome. After the fall of the Roman empire, for three centuries (sixth to ninth) it was a Byzantine dominion until 827 when the Arabs, arriving from the coasts of north Africa, occupied the island and divided it into three provinces.

It took the Arabs seventy-five years to conquer Sicily. They dominated it for more than two and a half centuries and lost it in thirty years. As time passed they became attached to the island and governed it so well that Sicily underwent a renaissance: it became a rich flourishing region and the center of trade in the Mediterranean ("white sea" they called it). The Arab rulers guaranteed freedom of worship, renewed agriculture, eliminated the great landed estates and introduced new crops such as citrus fruits, pistachios, mulberry, sugar cane and date palms. Palermo became a cosmopolitan cultural capital, the city of gardens, "of delights", with *hamam* and mosques, whose Koranic schools were centers for the study of science and law.

◄ Gelon, tyrant of Greek Syracuse.

Dynastic struggles or rivalries between the emirates weakened the power, and in the eleventh century the Arabs were defeated and driven out by the Normans. Robert the Guiscard (the Sly) and Roger I succeeded by Roger II continued to develop the island. They brought back Christianity, installed feudalism, and unified the kingdom with its various ethnic groups. Greek, Latin, Arab and Franco-Norman were all official languages. The poet Lucio Piccolo di Calanovella says – "the Normans defeated Islam, but with them Islam was reborn". Indeed they assimilated the techniques, customs and culture of Islam and employed their skilled workers to which the Palatine Chapel, the Cathedrals of Monreale and Cefalù bear witness.

With Frederick II (Hohenstaufen) of Swabia, crowned Holy Roman emperor in 1212, cultured and intelligent and defender of the arts, Sicily became one of the first modern states in Europe, a centralized state with a wise constitution, the *Liber Augustalis*. The nascent humanism was witness to the first *School of Poetics* in the vernacular, an *Institute of Medicine* and the *University*, and a capi-

◄ Kufic inscription of a verse of the Koran (Cathedral of Palermo).

tal, Palermo, with a court that was a center of art and culture between the East and the West, a hotbed for letters, philosophy, mathematics and science, attended by the most illustrious minds of the time. Frederick II guaranteed authority, affluence and peace during his thirty year reign and with his death in 1250 the golden age of Sicily came to a close. The slow decline of the island began with the Angevin, Aragonese and Bourbon occupations that followed. Confined and reduced to a region by distant empires, Sicily lost its independence and prestige.

In 1268 the Angevins moved the capital to Naples. They consolidated the feudal system, but were driven out by the people in 1282 (the famous revolt of the Sicilian Vespers) as a result of the increasingly heavy taxes exacted. Subsequently Sicily, joined to the crown of Aragon, was ruled by viceroys who favored the excessive

◄ Roger the II the Norman, the Knight of God.

power and luxury of the feudal barons and the aristocracy. In 1493 after fifteen centuries of living together, they turned out the Jews and introduced the *Inquisition*.

The discovery of the New World and its wealth, and the introduction of new foods and exotic spices also enfeebled Sicily, for the Mediterranean was no longer a strategic power. The Spanish, who never visited Sicily, with the exception of Charles V, subsequently ceded the island to the Savoy dynasty which in turn, in exchange for Sardinia, ceded it to the Austrians in 1720. In 1735 the island once more fell under the dominion of the Bourbon Spaniards, who taxed the life out of Sicily.

Later Sicily took up the cause of the Risorgimento, supporting Giuseppe Garibaldi who landed in Marsala

▼ The great Swabian emperor Frederick II.

on May 11, 1860 with his Thousand to free the island and reunite it to Italy in a single kingdom. Neither the Unity of Italy nor Fascism rescued Sicily from the impoverishment and isolation into which it had fallen. Many were the Sicilians, victims of the State and of history,

◀ Giuseppe Garibaldi, hero of the Italian Risorgimento.

who put their hopes in the Movement for the Autonomy of the island. In 1946 a special Statute granted Sicily regional autonomy and it has a Parliament of its own.

Today the island is deeply committed to the struggle against the age-old scourge, the Mafia, thanks also to courageous magistrates and the courage of the people themselves. Sicily is also doing its utmost for a rebirth and renewal, with the financial help of Europe and of tourism, which is becoming an increasingly important economic factor.

▼ Hall of the Parliament in the Norman Palace of Palermo.

▲ Temple E in Selinunte, built by the Greeks in harmony with the landscape.

● Art in Sicily

There is so much art in Sicily that one might almost think of the island as an open-air museum set into an extraordinary natural landscape. From prehistory to Greek art, from the great season of the Arabs and the Normans up to the richly creative Baroque and the nineteenth-century villas and gardens, Sicily offers highly original styles and works of art. Paleolithic Sicily is represented by the rock paintings (tuna fish, stags, dancing human figures) in the grottoes of Nicosia dell'Addaura and Levanzo in the Egadi Islands.

The Phoenicians have left tantalizing finds in that seductive strip of land of the isle of Mozia, the city they founded, with the *cothon*, the necropolis with the shrine: the *tophet* and the ten thousand objects including grinning masks, jewels, vases and utensils (Whitaker Museum on the island).

The fame of Sicily is due in particular to the many examples of Greek art and architecture now scattered throughout the land, ranging from the superb temples and theaters of the Valley of the Temples, to Selinunte, Segesta, Megara, Syracuse, and Taormina, a land that is more Greek than Greece itself. While the Romans reworked and adapted what the Greeks had created, their imposing public works such as the aqueduct of Termini Imerese as well as many magnificent country houses and dwellings with marvelous mosaics (Villa del Casale di Piazza Armerina) have survived the centuries. The Byzantines in turn transformed some of the Greek temples into the first basilicas: the Cathedral of Syracuse is the most outstanding example. Few traces remain of the essential, geometric and ornate Arab architecture, except for the decorations in the baths of Cefalà Diana, a portion of mosque inside San Giovanni degli Eremiti and the layout of the city. The Normans destroyed three hundred Arab mosques in a single night in Palermo.

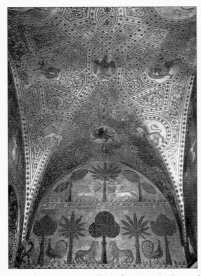

▲ Arab-Norman stylistic features in Roger's Room and in the Cloister of Monreale.

The glittering East combined with the austerity of the so-called "men of the north" produced the unique *Arab-Norman* civilization and style, "an artistic compromise" in the words of the historian Cesare Brandi, which bequeathed us with some of the finest religious and civil monuments in the world, such as the Palatine Chapel, the Cathedral of Monreale, Cefalù, the Cuba, the Zisa and the imposing castles.

With the exception of Francesco Laurana and Domenico Gagini (first in the line of a family of artists) who had trained with Brunelleschi in Florence, the Renaissance made little impact on Sicilian art.

The greatest Sicilian master in the figurative arts was Antonello da Messina, supreme painter of light and portraits, with masterpieces such as the *Annunciation*, the *Virgin Annunciate*, the *Portrait of a Man*, and the *Polyptych of Saint Gregory*, in various Sicilian museums. Other painters such as Caravaggio and Anthony Van Dyck also left conspicuous traces of their brief stays in Sicily.

After the terrible earthquake of 1693 which destroyed entire cities, under the Spanish viceroys Sicily became a great construction yard and churches, cathedrals, palaces and streets were rebuilt or built anew, prevalently in that most scenic, exuberant and

◄ The *Virgin Annunciate*, fifteenth-century masterpiece by Antonello da Messina (Regional Gallery in Palazzo Abatellis, Palermo).

► The Sicilian Baroque in the Cathedral of Modica.

imaginative of styles known as *Sicilian Baroque*. It is in these palaces and churches, in the cupids, the garlands, the anthropomorphic figures, that Sicily expressed its will to rise from the rubble of the earthquake in an opulent art well suited to the tastes of aristocrats and feudal barons. With great determination the Church and the religious orders supplied the best architects, almost all ecclesiastical, such as Angelo Italia, Giovanni Battista Vaccarini and Rosario Gagliardi, admittedly the genius of Sicilian Baroque. This was the heyday of stucco ornamentation, particularly by the Sicilian artist Giacomo Serpotta, who covered the walls of oratories and churches with his light and elegant tracery.

At the end of the nineteenth century Sicily welcomed the new *Art Nouveau* currents. The Basile family, father and son, created theaters, gardens and country houses, interpreting the expectations of the emerging Sicilian industrial bourgeoisie. Today Sicilian painting has achieved its apogee in the large brightly colored paintings by Renato Guttuso, native of Bagheria, who never forgot his Sicily even though he lived elsewhere.

▼ Chinoiserie and Art Nouveau in the Chinese Palace and in the Post Office of Palermo.

11

► Giovanni Verga
and Federico De Roberto.

▲ Luigi Pirandello.

● The Sicily of the Writers

Without the Sicilian writers and poets, Italian literature, one of the most noble and oldest in the European spirit, would not be nearly as rich as it is. Sicilian poetry was the first to be based on the vernacular rather than on Latin (thirteenth century) and from the late nineteenth century to the present the works of great authors have gone well beyond the confines of the island and of Italy. Two of them, Luigi Pirandello and Salvatore Quasimodo, were also the recipients of the Nobel Prize for Literature (respectively 1943 and 1959). They were preceded towards the end of the 19th century by other writers whose novels are still being read, by Giovanni Verga who wrote of the hard life and destiny of the fishermen and sulfur miners in his "I Malavoglia" (Under the Medlar Tree) and "Mastro Don Gesualdo", and by Federico De Roberto who realistically depicted the superstitions of the decadent Sicilian aristocracy in "The Viceroys". Luigi Pirandello with his subtle logic and extraordinary feel for drama is considered one of the greatest playwrights of twentieth century Europe. "Sei personaggi in cerca di autore" (Six characters in

◄ Elio Vittorini
and Vitaliano Brancati.

► Salvatore Quasimodo and Leonardo Sciascia.

search of an author), Henry IV, "Come tu mi vuoi", "Così è se vi pare" (That's How it Is, if You like) continue to be performed throughout the world, illustrating the existential and social crisis of modern man.

Sicily also produced great novels, especially in the twentieth century. Examples are Pirandello's "Il fu Mattia Pascal" (The Late Mattia Pascal), "Uno, nessuno e centomila". After World War II Elio Vittorini ("Conversations in Sicily") inaugurated epic literature of the "humiliated man". The Catanian Vitaliano Brancati ironically and proudly portrayed the vices of the Sicilian bourgeoisie and their so-called sexual conceits. Giuseppe Tomasi di Lampedusa painted a picture of the funereal and genial decadence of the Sicilian aristocracy in the middle of the 19th century in his novel "Il Gattopardo" (The Leopard), later turned into a film by Luchino Visconti. Leonardo Sciascia from Racalmuto was another great contemporary writer, gifted with an acute social sense and ingenious judicial fantasy. His novels "Il giorno della civetta" (The Day of the Owl), "Todomodo" (One Way or Another), "Gli zii di Sicilia" (Sicilian Uncles), present us with a raw cross-section of the mafia, justice and Sicilian society. Cur-

rently, next to novelists such as Gesualdo Bufalino ("Diceria dell'untore" or The Plague Sower) and Vincenzo Consolo, the television version of Andrea Camilleri's detective novels involving the police superintendent Montalbano have become particularly popular.

The Sicilian poets of today include the populist Ignazio Buttitta, who gives voice in dialect to the Sicilians without a voice, and Salvatore Quasimodo, who received the Nobel Prize in the 1950s, a mythical poet of Sicily's Greek nature (and a great translator of the ancient Greek Lyrics) and, later, of the human condition of modern man oppressed by contemporary power and violence ("Ed è subito sera", "La terra impareggiabile" or The Incomparable Earth and "La vita non è un sogno" or Life is not a Dream).

► Giuseppe Tomasi di Lampedusa.

► Pasta with sardines and the good Sicilian bread.

● Flavors of Sicily

While some of the Sicilian sweets and dishes could be thought of as typical of Sicily, such as *pasta con le sarde, pasta alla Norma* (Catania's homage to Vincenzo Bellini), or the *cassata* and the *cannoli*, you would be hard put to find a town that doesn't have a dish or sweet of its own for the holidays or Easter. In 330 B.C. the poet Archestratus of Gela extolled the Sicilian cuisine and cooks from here were often invited to Athens. The tradition of Sicilian gastronomy is Mediterranean with bread and pasta, introduced by the Greeks, or the *focaccia* favored by the Romans. Bread in Sicily can be in any shape or size: long, round, oval, black or white, with sesame or cumin or fennel seeds, but it must be fresh (bak-

eries are open even on holidays). A Sicilian can't eat without bread. Pasta, dry or freshly home-made, reigns over the table, served with vegetables, tomato or ragù sauce, with the tasty oil and bread crumbs known

▼ Rice balls, *panelle* and fried foods.

▲ The famous pistachios of Bronte and the sweet couscous.

as *cca muddica*, the Agrigento pesto made with pistachios (the gold of Bronte), or the delicate ravioli filled with ricotta and mint or the fried pasta with oranges.

Rice was introduced by the Arabs and is used for timbales, sweets and the famous *arancini*, deep-fried rice balls with saffron and meat sauce and *caciocavallo* cheese. The Arabs also introduced couscous as well as spices and in the area of Trapani, together with fish, it is one of the main dishes to which a festival has been devoted.

The sun-ripened Mediterranean vegetables are bursting with flavor. Eggplants and bell peppers, celery, tomatoes and a variety of sweet zucchini almost thirty centimeters long are all used together in the ever-present *caponata*, and every city or town has its own version. The zucchini leaves, called *tenerumi*, are also cooked.

The broad beans are good by themselves, as salad, or in a puree known as *maccu* made with sautéed chopped onions and tomatoes. Pine nuts, almonds, walnuts, raisins and pista-

chios, here growing in abundance, accompany both main dishes and sweets. The typical meat in the Sicilian cuisine is kid or lamb. Fish, as is natural for an island, plays a large part in the diet: swordfish and tuna fish, oven-baked, smoked, fried, with tomato, or grilled, in grape leaves Greek-style, or seasoned with a good *salmoriglio* sauce. Then there are the *sarde a beccafico*, with bread crumbs, raisins and orange juice, and the *sardines* and *squid*, up to the *baccalà* and *stoccafisso* (dried cod) introduced by the men of the north. The

► Swordfish.

15

◄▲ Marzipan sweets
and the famous Sicilian cannoli.

French introduced the braised and gratinéed onions as well as the custom of covering meat and certain vegetables with puff paste, like the *farsu magru*, rolls of meat filled with raisins, pine nuts, hard boiled eggs, and cheese.

Oranges are served as fruit but are also added to salads with fennel, olives, tomatoes, as well as sweets. Sicily is a master chef when it comes to sweets, with the *cassata*, the emir's dessert, a symbol of voluptuous food. The cassata was first created around the tenth century with the Arabs when a Saracen cook mixed ricotta and sugar in a copper tureen (hence the name *qas'at*), adding an apotheosis of candied fruit, sponge cake soaked in rum, and, with the Spanish, pieces of chocolate. The result is creamy with a delicate flavor and an intense aftertaste of fresh ricotta. The famous *cannoli*, like most of the Sicilian sweets, also use ricotta.

Frutta martorana known as the sweet with a celestial flavor – perhaps because it was created by the nuns in the convent la Martorana in Palermo – is prepared with almond paste and sugar and then colored. It is said that the nuns first made *frutta martorana* to decorate the trees in the garden for the visit of a bishop but that in 1575 this same bishop prohibited them from preparing sweets during Holy Week so they would not be distracted from their prayers.

▼ "Frutta martorana" and the cassata, the sweet symbol of Sicily.

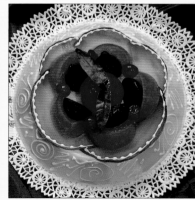

● Puppets and Carts, symbols of Sicily

The Sicilian puppets, actually marionettes, are known as "*pupi*" and are of wood, moved by strings, and represent sumptuously dressed knights and ladies of times past, with veils, swords and suits of armor, who act out, in stentorian voices and with cries and moans, stories of love and death, charming the popular imagination from tiny, magic stages. The beginnings of the *Opera dei Pupi* go way back, perhaps to right after the Middle Ages when the great romantic cycles of the paladins Orlando and Rinaldo and the beautiful Angelica enchanted the popular audiences of Europe. These stories found their way to Sicily in the nineteenth century and immediately interpreted the tragic and exuberant nature of the Sicilian temperament. The eternal struggle between good and evil has always been what theater is about, in a setting both magical and realistic with glittering tin swords and suits of armature in an exotic eastern ambience, with kings, knights and lovely maidens, and it has fascinated young and old.

The puppet theater exists almost everywhere in Sicily, but the original puppet theater must be seen in Palermo, its homeland, or in Catania where the *Teatro Stabile dell'Opera dei Pupi* has been established recently in the great complex of the Ciminiere, under the guidance of the dei Napoli family, puppeteers since 1921. The puppets of Catania can be distinguished from those of Palermo by their size. The former are larger, over a meter high, while those of Palermo are smaller and perhaps more articulated in their movements.

The magic created by these folk performances in the fragile puppet theaters spreads to the streets, above all for the feasts of the patron saints, the *sagras*, and other events with the appearance of the famous brightly painted "Sicilian carts", originally used for work, transporting grain, stones and household goods and now the colorful symbol of the island.

As time passed they became true works of art, on which various artisans worked – blacksmiths, decorators, carvers and painters. Every part of the cart was done with the utmost care, and finally painted in brilliant colors which varied from one part of Sicily to another and ranged from bright red to intense yellow to green, generally in striking combinations.

PALERMO

◄ Frederick II, "enlightened" sovereign of Sicily.

Punic, Greek, Roman, Byzantine, Arab, later Norman and Swabian, thirteen dominations in twenty-eight centuries. This succession of civilizations, peoples and history, left deep wounds, but also fascinating memories and treasures in Palermo, city of marvels, where everything lives together almost magically. The city casts its spell over visitors and accompanies them on their discovery of a Mediterranean city, with a pinch of the exotic, complex and dreamlike, regal and hybrid, exciting and mournful, miserable and noble, hospitable and diffident.

The overwhelming fragrance of jasmine and orange blossoms, oases of green palms, the aroma of *arancini* (fried rice balls), *panelle* and bread with the *meusa* (spleen) enchant the senses. Palermo is vermillion domes and austere cloisters, Baroque piazzas like city parlors, dark lanes, deteriorating palaces, ghostly reminders of a luxurious past that is gone forever, and colorful and noisy markets, reminiscent of an Arab *suq*. Reigning over it all is the slow hedonistic rhythm of the Near East, and the light, white and blinding, that takes on color when the sirocco blows relentlessly. Today things are changing. In the Babel of its historical center and the markets *Ballarò, Vucciria, Capo* and *Lattarini*, the beauty and

▼ Bird's eye view of the cove, with Monte Pellegrino in the background.

◄ A "sfincioni" stand at the Ballarò market.

soul of Palermo come to the fore and, despite neglect by the State and the arrogance of the Mafia, there is a renewed will for rebirth. Restoration, renovation, building, a new metro and the reopening of churches and palaces are signs of this change. With its million inhabitants (including the hinterland) Palermo is the capital of the region and fifth largest city in Italy. It is located on a bay, at the edge of the plain of the *Conca d'oro* or golden horn of plenty, no longer golden because of the shambles of the building boom. To the north is *Monte Pellegrino*, with the pilgrimage site of the **Shrine of Santa Rosalia**, patron saint of the Palermitani, on the promontory that Goethe described as "the loveliest in the world". Opulent, crowded, elegant Palermo, paradise of delights and gardens, compared by travelers to the legendary Cordoba and Baghdad, is the Islamic *Balarm* of the ninth-tenth century, second to Constantinople, affectionately called *al-Madinah* by the Arabs.

…"*If I have been driven from a paradise, how can I tell you what it's like?*…, wrote Ibn Hamdis, from his exile when in 1072 the Normans took Palermo from the Arabs after five months of tenacious resistance. The Normans made it a Christian city,

▼ The magnificent Baroque palaces in the scenic Piazza Quattro Canti.

▲ The monumental Porta Felice from the sea.

filling it with churches, convents and castles, governed it in the same way as the Islamic emirs, after destroying, in a single night by order of the Church three hundred mosques. Palermo today has practically nothing to testify to the Arab presence, except for a few ruins.

Around the thirteenth century with Frederick II of Swabia – the *Stupor Mundi* who made a State of Sicily – Palermo became one of the foremost courts in Europe, capital of letters and science, where the first school of Italian poetry known as the *Sicilian School* was born. Then came the Spanish domination.

Quattro Canti or **Piazza Vigliena** or **Teatro del Sole** is the spectacular Baroque piazza, symbol of Spanish power, with four palaces whose concave facades are adorned with statues. *Corso Vittorio Emanuele*, the old *Càssaro* (from the Arab *al Qasr*-fortezza), and *Via Maqueda*, meet here, dividing the city into four quarters: Albergheria, Kalsa, Vucciria and Capo.

To the left of the piazza is the **Albergheria** quarter, a name that refers to the many inns and hotels once there. The **Church of San Giuseppe dei Teatini** with a fine dome in green majolica tiles and with an abundance of frescoes inside by Guglielmo Borremans and Giuseppe Serpotta, dates to the seventeenth century. The sixteenth-century **Porta Nuova** with its

► The tiled dome of San Giuseppe dei Teatini.

▲◄ The Norman Palace,
the Pisan Tower and the Porta Nuova,
and view of Roger's Room.

In the eleventh century Emir *Assan Ben Alì* had a castle built on what was probably once a Punic fort, with four towers (the only one left is the **Pisan Tower**). In the twelfth century Roger II transformed it into a lavish royal residence, with a *harem* and the *tiraz*, the state textile workshops. After the death of Frederick II, the palace was abandoned. The Spanish preferred the imposing **Palazzo Steri** begun by Manfred I Chiaramonte in 1307, the decoration of which was finished in 1380. **Roger's Room** is on the second floor of what was once the *Joaria* tower with a plethora of gold mosaics with scenes of the hunt, animals and trees, created by the Arab-Byzantine workshops which

majolica gable, at the end of Corso Vittorio Emanuele, dominates *Piazza Vittoria*, with the lovely palm gardens of **Villa Bonanno** overlooked by the **Norman Palace**, seat of the Region of Sicily.

had worked on the magnificent Palatine Chapel, a wonder of Arab-Byzantine syncretism, a new style created by the 'men from the north', characteristic of medieval Sicily.

In the **Palatine Chapel**, with its eastern overtones, Islamic art survived as a style in the service of the new king (*basileus*). Roger II's jewel was built on a basilica plan in 1132 and consecrated in 1140. The nave is separated from the two side aisles by alternating columns of porphyry and Egyptian marble, with Corinthian

▼ The pulpit in the right aisle and the paschal candlestick in the Palatine Chapel.

▼ Close-up of the mosaic of the *Baptism of Saint Paul*.

▲ Detail of the wooden *muquarnas* ceiling in the Palatine Chapel with eight-pointed stars, symbol of the Cosmos.

capitals and Moorish ogee arches, crowned with a dome. The floor is in *pietre dure* mosaic and the upper walls are entirely covered with luminous gold mosaics depicting scenes and figures of the *Life of Christ, Saints Peter and Paul*, episodes from the *Acts of the Apostles and the Old Testament*. A splendid *Christ Pantokrator* blessing in the Byzantine manner is in the apse conch. In the bowl-shaped vault of the central cupola is another *Christ Pantokrator* with a closed book and *Angels and Archangels*.

The coffered wooden ceiling of the nave is a marvel of Arab art, a foretaste of Paradise, carved and decorated in *muqarnas*, with Kufic inscriptions and figures in the eight-pointed stars, Islamic symbols of the cosmos. The *royal throne* and the pulpit set on columns are also covered in mosaic inlays while the *Paschal candlestick* supported by lions is a splendid work by the stone-carvers of Palermo. The only purely Arab element is the **Crypt**, beneath the Palatine Chapel.

◀ The Crypt.

▲ View of the half-dome in the apse in the Palatine Chapel.

◄ The dome of Santa Caterina.

in a technique called *qubba*, with square ashlars and scarlet domes. The church has a nave only and three apse niches, and is entered through a fine **Cloister** in a fragrant garden of orange trees, jasmine, prickly pears and exotic plants that brings to mind the antique oasis of delights.

Like a humming *suq* the market of **Ballarò** (from the Arab *al Bhalharà*) is the heart of the narrow quarter that reaches to the seventeenth-century **Church of the Carmine** in the square of the same name, with a majolica dome, stucco decor by Giuseppe and Giacomo Serpotta and a fine painting of *Saint Andrea Corsini* by Pietro Novelli. Palermitan Baroque reaches its zenith in the Jesuit **Casa Professa** or **Church of the Gesù**, overflowing with polychrome marble inlays, stat-

Together with those of San Cataldo, the red domes of the **Church of San Giovanni degli Eremiti**, the king's favorite, are the principal elements in Palermo's skyline. In 1132 he had it built on a mosque by Arab craftsmen

▼ The cloister of the Church of San Giovanni degli Eremiti.

▲ ▶ Pretoria Fountain (or of Shame) and detail depicting the Oreto River.

ues and stuccoes of cupids, garlands and angels by Giacomo Serpotta on the dome and in the nave and two aisles, of the eighteenth century. The **Cloister** is not to be missed.

The **Kalsa** (*al Halisah*, the elect), citadel of the Emir and the bureaucrats, is the quarter to the right of *Via Maqueda* with the scenic **Pretoria Fountain** at the center of *Piazza Pretoria*. Gods, monsters, animals, cupids and statues in white marble adorn the elliptical Mannerist fountain by the Florentine sculptor Francesco Camilleri. Too many nudes for the citizens of Palermo, who named it the fountain of shame. In 1573 it was bought for twenty thousand *scudi* by the Palermo Senate as a symbol of power over the viceroy. The **Palazzo Senatorio** or **delle Aquile**, on the square, is now Palermo's City Hall. The immense sixteenth-century **Church of Santa Caterina**– with the statue of the saint over the portal by Gagini and lavish decorations in the interior – overlooks Piazza Bellini which has two pearls of Arab-Norman architecture facing each other: the Churches of San Cataldo and La Martorana or Santa Maria dell'Ammiraglio.

▲ The Churches of the Martorana and of San Cataldo.

The cubic and severe **Church of San Cataldo** dates to 1160. It has three red domes, and crenellations and blind arcading along the exterior with a fine mosaic floor in the interior with a nave and two aisles. **La Martorana** or **Santa Maria dell'Ammiraglio** of the twelfth century stands in one of the most densely populated areas of Palermo and was named for Eloisa Martorana, who founded the neighboring Bene-

◄▲ The fascinating interior of the Church of the Martorana and mosaic depicting *Roger II Crowned by Christ.*

► The Ball Room of Palazzo Gangi.

dictine convent. The church is flanked by a four-story square bell tower, erected by Admiral George of Antioch, a Syrian Christian Arab in the service of Roger II. Restored frequently over the centuries, the church is lavishly faced with twelfth-century Byzantine mosaics: *Christ Pantokrator with Angels and Archangels* dominates the center of the dome and along the walls are the *Birth of Christ*, the *Death of the Virgin*, a curious *Mary spinning*, and the famous mosaic of the theocrat *Roger Crowned by Christ* and not by the Pope.

Lining the street on the way to the Church of the Magione are the patrician residences of the proud Gattopardi family: **Palazzo Comitini**, **Santa Croce-Sant'Elia** or **Palazzo Fi**langeri Cutò and then **Palazzo Gangi-Valguarnera** where Luchino Visconti shot some of the scenes of the film *The Leopard (Il Gattopardo)* and the **Palazzo Ajutamicristo** with a fine Gothic loggia.

The charming **Church of the Magione** or **Basilica of the Santissima Trinità,** founded in 1150 by the king's chancellor Matteo d'Aiello for the Cistercian monks, is Arab-Norman in style. The facade has three tiers of pointed arches. Inside is an old *Sinopia of Christ*. The lovely cloister, with double pointed arches resting on twin columns, is part of the original Cistercian monastery.

The former church of **Santa Maria dello Spasimo** in the heart of the *Kalsa* is a center for cultural activities. It

◄ The facade of the Church of the Magione.

◄ The roofless Church of Santa Maria dello Spasimo.

lost its roof in the bombings of World War II but still has the three aisles and cross vaulting. The **Botanical Gardens**, one of the oldest in Italy, and the eighteenth-century **Villa Giulia** gardens, behind the complex of the Spasimo, are the exotic paradises of Palermo. The walk or Passeggiata della Marina, now the *Foro Italico*, through palm gardens is splendid. The wall at the end is known as the **Mura delle cattive** and was where the widows used to pass their time.

The **Church of Santa Maria degli Angeli** (sixteenth cent.) known as **La Gancia** is in the historical *Via Alloro*. Originally built by the Franciscans as a hospice but then modified, the small church contains interesting works surrounded by Serpotta's white stuccoes. One of these is the sixteenth-century *Marriage of the Virgin* by the sculptor Vincenzo da Pavia. Next to it is the **Regional Gallery of Sicily**, housed in the magnificent *Palazzo Abatellis*, a Gothic-Catalan building by Matteo Carnelivari. On its two floors the museum contains numer-

▼ The *Triumph of Death* (Regional Gallery of Sicily).

ous works of art from the thirteenth to the seventeenth century. In the sculpture section note particularly the *sarcophagus of Cecilia Aprile* and the lovely *bust of Eleonora of Aragon* by Francesco Laurana, considered one of this sculptor's masterpieces. The same room contains the famous awe-inspiring fifteenth-century fresco of the *Triumph of Death* by an unknown artist, from Palazzo Sclafani in Palermo. Death in the guise of a knight looses his arrows against the rich. The *Madonna del Latte* by Domenico Gagini and sculptures of the *Virgin* by the Gagini family are lovely. The thirteenth-century Byzantine mosaic with a *Madonna Odigitria* (she who indicates the way) is by an unknown artist. On the second floor, devoted to painting, the jewel of the museum is the famous fifteenth-century *Virgin Annunciate* by Antonello da Messina, and three saints by the same artist: *Gregory, Jerome* and *Augustine*. Among the paintings of Flemish school the finest is the *Malvagna Triptych*, by Jean Gossaert known as Mabuse, with a *Madonna and Child with Angels*.

▼ The famous *Virgin Annunciate* by Antonello da Messina (Regional Gallery of Sicily in Palazzo Abatellis).

The lively *Piazza Marina* – with the nineteenth-century Garibaldi gardens designed in 1863 by Filippo Basile and which contains a gigantic *ficus magnoloides* or banyan tree – was once the theater for the *auto da fe* trials for since 1601 the Sant'Offizio or Spanish Inquisition had its headquarters in the somber **Palazzo Steri** built in 1307 by the powerful Chiaramonte family.

◄ The Art Nouveau shop window of a bakery at Capo.

Santa Maria della Catena (16th cent.) is the Gothic-Catalan church at the top of the staircase, with a loggia with three arches decorated with sculpture by Vincenzo Gagini; the church takes its name from the chain (*catena*) which closed the harbor.

The **Oratory of San Lorenzo** and the **Church of San Francesco d'Assisi** are close to each other. The oratory, built by the company of Saint Francis in 1569, has a luminous interior with a magnificent display of stuccoes and statues by Giacomo Serpotta. The church is older but has been renovated frequently. The facade mirrors the saint's sobriety, with a fourteenth-century portal and a fine rose-window, while the three-aisled interior with chapels is embellished with sculpture by Serpotta and the school of Gagini.

The legendary **Focacceria di San Francesco** on the square is well worth a pause to try some of their *arancini*, *panelle* and above all the *sfincione*, the pizza of Palermo.

Among the web of labyrinthine lanes and with its own market, crowded

▼ Remains of frescoes in the Church of San Francesco.

▲ The lush English Gardens.

with Palermitani eating roast meat as they stroll along, is the **Capo,** the quarter where the opera theater of Palermo stands, the **Teatro Massimo**, restored and recently reopened after twenty-five years. The theater separates and connects old Palermo to the Palermo of the wealthy bourgeoisie and their elegant Art Nouveau residences on **Via Ruggero Settimo** and **Viale della Libertà**, known for their fashion boutiques, historical book stores, antique dealers, luxurious and modern cafes.

The thirteenth-century **Church of Sant'Agostino**, built by the Chiaramonte and Sclafani families, has a splendid rose-window on the facade and fine stuccoes by Giacomo Serpotta inside.

▼ The Teatro Massimo.

▲▼ The south side and the apses of the Cathedral.

And now for the golden-hued principal church, the majestic **Cathedral** of Palermo, dedicated to Our Lady of the Assumption, with its many memories and tombs. The mortal remains of Constance of Aragon and Henry VI, Frederick II of Swabia and Constance of Altavilla, Peter of Aragon and Roger II rest in large sarcophagi in the Cathedral. Built in only two years in the late twelfth century by the bishop Gualtiero Offamilio, the Cathedral sums up various styles and the alterations are evident.

The Gothic-Catalan porch, with three ogee arches and a decorated tympanum, is framed by two small towers decorated with paired columns and blind ogee arcading. Pointed arches join the bell tower to the church, while

◀ The Crown of Constance (Cathedral Treasury).

▲ The red porphyry sarcophagus of Frederick II.

the dome is an eighteenth-century addition. Entrance is through the fifteenth-century portal by the sculptor Antonio Gambara, above which is a twelfth-century niche lined with a mosaic of the *Madonna and Child*. The Latin-cross interior has three aisles and three apses. Sculptures by Francesco Laurana and Antonio Gagini embellish the transept and the presbytery with the *bishop's throne*. To the right of the presbytery is the **Chapel of Santa Rosalia**, the beloved patron saint of the Palermitani who saved them from the plague in 1624 and to whom a six-day festival is dedicated in July and a pilgrimage to the grotto in September. The chapel contains a finely chased silver *urn* with the relics of the saint. Ivory, gold work, objects in silver and enamel, and Byzantine icons are to be found in the Cathedral **Treasury**, while the newly restored **Diocesan Museum** – closed for the last twenty years – is once more open in the fifteenth-century *Bishop's Palace* opposite the Cathedral.

▶ The feast of the Santuzza and the silver urn of Santa Rosalia, in the Chapel that bears her name.

▲▶ View of room I and *Abraham and the Three Angels* by the Maestro delle Incoronazioni (Diocesan Museum).

Thirteen rooms on two floors house numerous paintings, sculpture and decorative arts from twelfth- to nineteenth-century Sicily. The Norman-Swabian period (room I) is represented by Madonnas such as the splendid *Madonna della Spersa* (13th cent.) and the mosaic *Praying Madonna* dating to the twelfth century. Scenes from the life of Saint Rosalia are depicted on the ivory medallions in the frame of a panel depicting *Saints Oliva, Elia, Venera and Rosalia.* The seventeenth-century *Pietà* that dominates room XII is by Pietro Novelli while works by the sculptors Antonello and Domenico Gagini and Francesco Laurana are in room VIII. Room X is dedicated to works by the Neapolitan painter Mario di Laurito with views of the city, such as the painting of *Palermo Saved from the Plague* commissioned in 1530 by the Senate of Palermo. *Palermo Liberated from the Plague* on the other hand, a splendid view with the most important monuments of the city, is by Simone de Wobreck.

The **Vucciria**, the most glorious and picturesque market and quarter of the harbor of Cala di Palermo takes its name from the French *Boucherie*, or butcher's shop, and was celebrated in a famous painting by the Sicilian artist Renato Guttuso. The market is not what it once was, but it is still a place where the Palermitani, who love their fresh octopus, and curious tourists go. Two bell towers, a Baroque facade and sober decorations inside the **Church and Convent of San Domenico** are the scenic elements of

► Van Dyck's altarpiece in the Oratory of San Domenico.

the *pantheon* of the glories of Palermo who rest here, including the statesman Francesco Crispi.

The seventeenth-century **Oratory of San Domenico** is a riot of works of art: stuccoes and allegorical sculpture by Serpotta and Gagini, the *Mysteries of the Rosary* along the walls, painted by Pietro Novelli and Luca Giordano and an altarpiece by Van Dyck, a *Madonna of the Rosary with the patrons and Saint Domenic*. After the Fascist **Post Office**, comes the sixteenth-century **Oratory of the SS. Rosario di Santa Cita** or **Zita**, a masterpiece by a mature Serpotta, with a Baroque elegance and airy passion. Devotion and allegory in stucco alternate along the walls up to the back of the nave with its splendid *Battle of Lepanto*.

▼ The Oratory of Santa Cita, masterpiece by Giacomo Serpotta.

◄ One of the metopes from the Temples of Selinunte ("Antonino Salinas" Archaeological Museum).

pheus taming the wild animals and *Hercules killing the stag.*

There are some true architectural jewels in the Arab-Norman style in the **outskirts of Palermo** in the *Gennat al ard*, the "paradise on earth", an enchanting park and a series of gardens of Islamic inspiration, where the Normans, the 'men from the north', who had adopted that sublime taste for the pleasure of living, recreated their terrestrial paradise, the magical *Genoard*, cradle of indolence and pleasures of court, such as the **Zisa** (*al Aziz* the splendid), royal residence begun in 1165 by William I the Bad and finished by his son William II, known as the Good, the *Musta'izz* (eager for glory) as he had himself called. At night, the skilful lighting reveals the long-gone mysteries of al-Aziz, the place of plea-

Behind the oratory, in *Via Bara all'Olivella*, the former **Convent of Sant'Ignazio** houses the rich **Antonino Salinas Archaeological Museum** which dates to 1866 and the amount of material housed on the three floors of the former convent makes it one of the most important in Italy: archaeological finds from the sea of Sicily, objects of daily use, Phoenician, Greek, Roman and Egyptian sculpture, such as the *Stone of Palermo*, an extraordinary fragment of a hieroglyphic inscription of the five Egyptian dynasties. And then the fifth-century BC *sarcophagi, lionhead rainspouts* from the temple of Victory of Himera, or the splendid *metopes* from the temples of Selinunte and then *cippi*, funerary *stelae* of Etruscan origin and sarcophagus *lids with the image of the deceased.* Of particular note are the third-century BC *mosaics of Piazza Vittoria* with *Or-*

► *Hercules Killing the Stag* ("Antonino Salinas" Archaeological Museum).

▲ ▶ The Zisa
and the Room of the Fountain.

◀ The fascinating *muqarnas*
decorations inside the Zisa.

sure, mirrored in a pool in the midst of luxuriant gardens. The palace, facing the sea to receive the breeze, with three tiers of blind arcading, is a rectangular building twenty-five meters high and thirty-five wide with two square towers. The atmosphere in these large rooms with cross vaulting, oriental Corinthian columns, Arabian *muqarnas* wall decor is fabulous, as in the enchanting *Room of the Fountain* with its mosaics and grooved stones for water. The *harem* was on the first floor.

▲▼ The Cuba and the Church of San Giovanni dei Lebbrosi.

The **Cuba** or *Solatio* was another pleasure palace, surrounded by water in the large *Genoard* park, now incorporated into military barracks. This Fatimite architecture with pointed arches of varying widths was built by William II in 1180. Giovanni Boccaccio chose the rooms of the Cuba in his tales of the *Decameron* as setting for the love story of Restituta and Gian di Procida (sixth story on the fifth day).

Surrounded by palm trees, the austere **Church of San Giovanni dei Lebbrosi** with fine red domes and three apses dates to 1070 and is the oldest Arab-Norman monument in Palermo.

Not far off are the famous **Capuchin**

► ▼ The Chinese Palace and the splendid Italian style gardens.

Catacombs, a haunting spectacle of eight thousand well-dressed mummies, the mortal remains of the religious and bourgeois citizens of Palermo. When the writer Guy de Maupassant, was touring Sicily and saw them he fainted.

Not far off is the **Maredolce** or **Castello della Favara**, a scenic palace with its walls painted gold, in a paradisiacal landscape, below the mountain and on the river, surrounded by some of the loveliest gardens and created for the pleasure and delight of the sultan Giafar and then the Great Count Roger.

The orientalizing **Chinese Palace** in the surroundings of the **Parco della Favorita** is completely different in style. It was the residence of Ferdinand I Bourbon, king of the two Sicilies, and Maria Carolina, built in 1799 by Venanzio Marvuglia, and with a splendid hidden Italian style garden in addition to its riot of frescoes and spiral staircases. Also in the Parco della Favorita is the **Pitrè Ethnographical Museum** with interesting collections of objects and documents that bear witness to the Sicilian temperament and folklore.

Province of Palermo

■ Monreale

Defined "glorious" by Francesco Gabrielli, the great orientalist, in one of his essays, the Cathedral of Monreale is the peak of Arab-Norman architecture. It was founded around 1174 by King William II the Good, in honor of the Madonna. The incredible blaze of light and beauty lends the church a solemn majesty, stylistically the synthesis of Romanesque-Byzantine building structures and with six thousand three hundred and forty square meters of mosaics and exotic and superb Islamic decorations created by Moorish craftsmen who succeeded in capturing the light of the divine in their bare stone traceries.

William II of Altavilla (whose remains together with those of his wife Margherita, rest in the Cathedral) built it on the hill *Mons Regalis* – regal mountain – a strategic peak that dominated the Conca d'Oro and the Oreto River. The site was surrounded by a hunting reserve for Arab, and later Norman, notables.

Still today the panorama from here over Palermo, up to the sea and that famous valley of oranges, the Conca d'Oro, is breath-taking.

Monreale, a lively suburb eight kilometers from Palermo, presents the visitor with its narrow streets and square piazzas, pastry shops and small restaurants, dry fruit and seed stands and endless souvenir shops. The vital lymph of Monreale are the many tourists who come every year to visit its superb **Cathedral,** built together with the Royal Palace and the Episcopal Palace in only ten years, an affirmation of Norman power. King William the Good spared no expense and then entrusted it to the

▼ The facade
of the Cathedral of Monreale.

care of the Benedictines who are still there and for whom the **Abbey** was built. Outside the *apses*, facing east, are decorated with pointed arches and ocher-colored inlays which lighten their mass.

Two towers frame the eighteenth-century *facade* with a porch of three arches sheltering the *Gate of Paradise*, the bronze doors sculptured in 1186 by Andrea Bonanno from Pisa, with 42 panels of biblical episodes and with a *griffin* and a *lion*, symbols of Norman power, on the lower part.

▼ The mosaic of *Christ Pantokrator* in the apse of the nave.

◀ Detail of the mosaics of the *Creation*.

The three-aisled interior is immense, with 18 columns with Roman capitals and ogee arches separating the nave from the aisles. The floor is in precious marble mosaic and the wooden ceiling is decorated with *muqarnas* (honeycomb compartments and stalactites). Mosaics with the *stories of the Old and New Testaments* run along the upper part of the nave while on the walls of the aisles are scenes from the *Gospels* and the *Acts of the Apostles*. Other mosaics narrate stories of *Mary Magdalene*, the *Madonna Odigitria* (she who indicates the way) and events in the life of the king: *William II offering the Virgin the model of the Cathedral* and *William II Crowned by Christ*. The mosaic apotheosis is in the vault of the apse where the figure of *Christ Pantokrator* (the

omnipotent) blessing in the Greek manner looks down while below are the *Apostles* and the *Virgin and Child enthroned*, with the Greek word *Panacrontas* (all saint).

The Arab voices celebrating the greatness of God are most powerful in the **Cloister**, on the right side of the Cathedral, the largest and most representative of the twelfth century.

Small double ogee arches, supported by two hundred and twenty-eight paired columns with capitals decorated with figures and friezes no two of which are alike, elegantly scan

▶ *William II offering the model of the Cathedral to the Madonna.*

▲ ▼ The east apses of the Cathedral and the Benedictine Cloister.

the rhythm on four sides. The imaginative and incredibly light movement culminates in the small square **Chiostrino** (little cloister) with three arches per side, at the center of which is the splendid fountain with its stylized palm shaft.

The **Monastery of San Martino alle Scale** dates to the fifteenth century. It dominates the complex of Monreale from a distance of ten kilometers and was rebuilt on the foundations of a church and monastery from the time of Gregory the Great. The splendid frescoes inside by the seventeenth-century painter Pietro Novelli, a native son of Monreale, are not to be missed.

Piana degli Albanesi

Piana degli Albanesi is a town of six thousand inhabitants, a sort of amphitheater between the dam of the same name and Mount La Pizzuta. It is one of the five Albanian communities in Sicily, founded in the fifteenth century by Albanians who had fled the Balkans after the Ottoman Turk invasion. For five centuries these people, who live on agriculture and embroidery, have kept their national cultural, linguistic and religious identity alive, with fascinating rites, liturgy and traditions, with pageants and colorful costumes which reach their apex at Epiphany, on the feast day of the patron saint,

Saint Mary Odigitria, and at Easter and in baptisms and weddings when it is traditional to eat the famous *ricotta cannoli* which – say the Sicilians – are the best on the island.

Not to be missed is the splendid *Iconostasis* with the image of the *Odigitria* brought here by Albanian exiles in the fifteenth century, in the Orthodox **Church of Santa Maria Odigitria** on *Piazza Vittorio Emanuele*, heart of the historical center. The **Chiesa Madre of San Demetrio** is covered with frescoes by Pietro Novelli. The **Church of San Giorgio**, the oldest in town, was renovated in the eighteenth century. The reliefs of the *Martyrdom of Saint George* on the iconostasis are quite elaborate.

Objects and tools of the Albanian peasant and folklore tradition and splendid traditional costumes with their pure gold embroideries are on view in the **Anthropological Museum**.

◄ ▼ Typical costumes still used and view of the town.

■ Cefalà Diana

Cefalà Diana is a village of Arab origins, and barely a thousand souls live in the square one-story houses scattered on the slope of a hill. This is the only place in Sicily that still has truly Arab architectural elements: the Turkish baths and the castle.

Overlooking the village is the **Castle** with a three-story tower and crenellations. It has been completely restored and was one of the many lookout fortresses on the roads that led to Palermo.

The Baths consist of a rectangular building with five entrances and a single barrel-vaulted room with three ogee arches with round air ducts; the ablution basins are on two levels and almost completely sunk into the ground. A series of Kufic inscriptions run along the outer walls. Water at a temperature of thirty-eight degrees C ran into the basins from the springs in the neighboring limestone rocks of Pizzo Chiarastella. Today thanks to the many springs that gush from the rocks the entire area has been set aside as a **Nature Reserve**.

▼ The Baths of Cefalà Diana.

▲ ◄ Saracen tower and majolica tiles in the Cappella Bianchi in Corleone.

■ Corleone

The town of Corleone lies in a bowl in the midst of a splendid landscape: fertile countryside, limestone rocks and plenty of water. Inhabited in prehistoric times, since the Arab domination people have tenaciously held on to their peasant traditions. The name Corleone is known throughout the world, thanks to *The Godfather,* the film on the Mafia. In virtue of this "glory" many curious tourists arrive every year as do couples who want to get married in this unusual locality, now actually full of hardworking people.

Scenically the town is dominated by the forts of **Castello Soprano** with its **Saracen Tower**, and **Castello Sottano**, now a monastery of Friars Minor.

Not to miss in Corleone is the **Chiesa Madre** founded around the year Thousand, dedicated to *Saint Martin* and frequently remodeled in the course of the centuries. Inside is an altarpiece of *Saint Francis of Assisi* by Pietro Novelli and a splendid wooden *Crucifix* of Byzantine times. A painting of *St. John the Evangelist on the island of Patmos* by Giuseppe Velasquez is in the seventeenth-century **Church of Santa Rosalia**, while interesting majolica tiles cover the floor of the small **Church of the Bianchi**.

■ Palazzo Adriano

The art critic Vittorio Sgarbi called Palazzo Adriano, founded by Albanian refugees in 1488 in the green valley of the Sosio River, "the loveliest of the small towns of Sicily". The Sicilian film director Giuseppe Tornatore chose it for his film *Nuovo Cinema Paradiso* which won an Oscar, and brought fame to the town – the imaginary Giancaldo of the film. *Piazza Umberto* is an immense square for a town as small as Palazzo Adriano, oval and paved in porphyry and overlooked by the two finest **churches**: the sixteenth-century **Santa Maria Assunta**, Greek rite, housing a fine *Crucifix* by Marabitti, and the eighteenth-century **Santa Maria del Lume** of Latin rite.

A red dome rises up over the bell tower of the sixteenth-century stone **Church of San Nicolò** that stands in the upper city, where the ruins of a fourteenth-century **Castle** also stand next to a tower from the time of Frederick.

■ Petralia Soprana and **Petralia Sottana**

Two vacation towns in the midst of the rock outcrops of the Madonie, in an uncontaminated nature paradise and with a view that goes all the way to Mount Etna. At a thousand one hundred meters above sea level Petralia Soprana is the highest town in the Madonie. Below, on the left of the Imera River, is Petralia Sottana. They are three kilometers apart but share their history of dominations and feuds, the same houses in grey stone with red geraniums on the balconies, wrought iron street lamps and windows. The economy of the two towns is based on the working of wrought iron and the collecting of manna, which does not come down from the sky, but is the lymph of the flowering ash trees, the only ones in the Mediterranean, growing in a hundred hectares on the Madonie. In Petralia Soprana, where the seventeenth-century painter Fra' Umile

▼ The nature paradise of the Madonie.

◀ Manna tree
and collecting manna.

The **Chiesa Madre** in **Petralia Sottana** da Petralia was born, there are two **churches** to see: the **Matrice** and that of **Santa Maria di Loreto**. The first, with a fine Baroque porch with paired columns and a bell tower, contains a wooden *Crucifix* by Fra' Umile da Petralia and in the sacristy, enclosed in a case, is the only example of an Arab candelabrum. In the Greek-cross church of Santa Maria di Loreto, there is a fine fifteenth-century marble *icon*.

is the most interesting religious building. It dates to the sixteenth-century but was altered in the seventeenth. Inside, in addition to marble sculpture of the school of Gagini, there is a fifteenth-century *Triptych* by an unknown artist.

A magnificent sixteenth-century *altarpiece* with twenty-three blue-ground panels narrating *episodes from the life of Christ* is in the **Church of the SS. Trinità**.

▼ The charming panorama of Petralia Sottana.

▲ ▶ The harbor of Cefalù and view of the Cathedral.

■ Cefalù

Cefalù, one of the most pleasant and fascinating seacoast cities of Sicily with red-roofed houses in yellow stone, is located on a long narrow bay washed by the Tyrrhenian sea, at the foot of an imposing fortress, suspended, as it were, between the rock and the sea. It counts fifteen thousand inhabitants and has a picturesque small harbor.

Built around its Cathedral, its symbol, Cefalù is a favorite seaside resort for international society and bourgeois tourism. It has well-equipped beaches of golden sand, small bays set between reefs (splendid those in the area of the *Kalura*) and excellent restaurants serving seafood and traditional cuisine.

For Diodorus Siculus what the Greeks called *Kephaloidion* was already inhabited in 396 BC and even earlier by the Siculi. In 858 it became *Gaflundi* for the Arabs, but Cefalù owes its rebirth and fame to the Normans who built the Cathedral, the first church of Arab-Norman Christianity after the conquest. Built between 1131 and 1240, it was begun as a result of a vow Roger II made when he was in danger of being shipwrecked. It was also to be the *pantheon* of the Altavilla dynasty.

The **Cathedral** is visible from every corner of the city and from the sea. It stands on the square of the same name in the historical center, surrounded by fine palaces and churches and a labyrinth of streets and lanes.

◄ *Portrait of an Unknown Man* by Antonello da Messina (Mandralisca Museum).

portal, the **Porta Regum** or King's Gate, richly carved in marble, leads into the interior with pointed arches and columns separating the side aisles from the nave. It is a gleaming glitter of gold mosaics that run along the walls and the presbytery. There is something sublime in the imposing *Christ Pantokrator* in the apse as he gazes down with melancholy eyes and raises his hand in blessing.

Of particular note in the presbytery is a fourteenth-century *Crucifix* painted on both sides, while the twelfth-century **Cloister** still has parts of the twin-columned portico. The **Osterio Magno**, in Corso Ruggero, royal residence and later winter dwelling for the Ventimiglia family, is now an exhibition space for contemporary art.

Two imposing square bell towers, with two-light and one-light openings, frame the fifteenth-century portico with its three arches by Ambrogio da Como on the facade. The entrance

▼ The mosaic of *Christ Pantokrator* in the Cathedral apse.

▲ The sea of Cefalù seen from the Rocca.

Opposite the Cathedral is the **Mandralisca Museum**, the pride of Cefalù with its precious collections of antique books, coins, kraters, including the *Tunny Krater* of the fourth century BC, Greek vases from the seventh century BC and theater masks as well as in important **Picture Gallery** which contains Antonello da Messina's wonderful "*Portrait of an Unknown Man*". A climb up to the **Rocca di Cefalù** is particularly rewarding, with its extraordinary panorama of the city and green sea. In addition to the fortifications, there are ruins of the megalithic ninth-century BC **Temple of Diana** as well as of Greek and Byzantine structures.

In the nearby **GIBILMANNA** at the top of Monte Sant'Angelo one must see the twelfth-century **Shrine of Gibilmanna**, destroyed by the Arabs and then rebuilt, one of the most important sites of the Marian cult in Sicily and with a constant flow of pilgrims. The name comes from the Arab *gebel* which means mountain and from the *manna*, the lymph that was and still is gathered from the flowering ash trees.

► Altar of the Madonna in the Shrine of Gibilmanna.

■ Himera

Portions of walls, the vestiges of three **temples** and the terrace of the imposing Doric **Temple of Victory** built in the fifth century to celebrate the Greek victory over the Carthaginians, and the **necropolis** are all that remain of the glorious city of Himera, named after the nymph *Himera*. Stesichorus, one of the major Siciliote poets, was born here. It was founded in 648 BC by Greeks from Syracuse as an outpost against the Carthaginians who then razed it to the ground in revenge in 409 BC in Hannibal's famous battle.

There is an **Antiquarium** in the archaeological site where all the finds from the excavation campaigns are stored. The lion-head water spouts to channel the rain water from the roof are quite picturesque.

■ Termini Imerese

Termini Imerese is a city that stretches out along the Tyrrhenian coast at the center of the Gulf, from Capo Zafferano to Cefalù. The three thousand inhabitants live from fishing and industry in a city that in the last twenty years has become an industrial center. The spectacular panorama along the coast where modern Termini Imerese has developed has been spoiled by factories, while the old city is perched up above

▲▶ The Temple of Victory at Himera and the Cornelian Aqueduct at Termini Imerese.

on the slopes of Mount San Calogero.

The city is famous for its carnival, one of the most spectacular and richest in Sicily, which attracts many tourists each year. The city was founded in the eighth century BC and then was a point of reference for the exiles of the nearby Himera, destroyed by the Carthaginians (409 BC). Termini Imerese was prosperous under Roman domination when the *Thermae Himerenses* were developed, hot springs at a temperature of forty degrees C which Pindaro called "hot springs of the Nymphs", beneficial then and now in curing arthritis.

The **Amphitheater**, the walls of a **Basilica** in the public park of **Villa Palmieri** and the **Cornelian Aque-**

► The Cathedral of Caccamo.

duct bear witness to its fortunes under Roman domination.

The heart of the historical center of the upper city, in a maze of lanes continuously going up and down, is the seventeenth-century **Cathedral** on Piazza del Duomo, painted pink and renovated in Baroque times. The facade is decorated with sixteenth-century statues by Bartolomeo Berrettaro and works by Ignazio Marabitti, Pietro Ruzzolone and Giorgio da Milano are inside.

The **Municipal Museum** with a fine collection of archaeological finds is housed in the rooms of the fourteenth-century former hospital. Included are prehistoric and Roman finds, objects from the excavations of Himera and inscriptions, coins and paintings and Flemish tapestries. Worthy of note is a second-century BC marble bust of a Roman woman.

■ Caccamo

C accamo is a pleasant town in the midst of softly rolling hills. It has eight thousand inhabitants and is known for its twenty churches and above all for its impregnable **Castle** on a spur of rock that overlooks the town. Built by the Normans, it was frequently modified, first by the Chiaramonte and then by the De Spuches families. The castle in white stone is considered one of the most significant of the Sicilian Middle Ages: crenellated with two-light openings and imposing towers and enclosed by walls.

There are one hundred and thirty rooms and one of these, the *Room of the Conspiracy*, with a splendid coffered ceiling, was witness in 1160 to the rebellion of the barons led by Matteo Bonello against William the Bad, a story told in the murals in Caccamo. The **Cathedral** or **Chiesa Matrice** dedicated to Saint George is also Norman and was built around the year thousand and restored at various times. A bas relief over the portal on the facade depicts *Saint George killing the dragon* while inside there is a fine baptismal font by the sculptor Domenico Gagini.

The polychrome majolica floor depicting *a ship surrounded by angels, fruit and flowers* in the **Church of San Benedetto alla Badia** is magnificent. The **Church of the Santissima Annunziata** contains stuccoes by Serpotta and an *Annunciation* by Borremans.

Bagheria

A fertile countryside and the surviving orange groves of the Conca d'Oro lie behind this city on the Tyrrhenian sea. The aristocracy and the land-owning nobility built their magnificent Baroque palaces here from the late seventeenth to the early twentieth century. The curlicues, garlands, anthropomorphic figures and animals with which they are overloaded gave free rein to the creative fantasy of the owners. These villas, which attract any number of visitors, now belong to and are identified with Bagheria.

Now a city-district of Palermo, only fourteen kilometers away, cement has done away with many of the splendid parks and gardens of exotic plants and the citrus groves that filled the

◄ Renato Guttuso.

sea air of Bagheria with their fragrance, a sort of paradise for the patrician families of Palermo fleeing the oppressing sultry heat of the capital.

The twentieth-century painter Renato Guttuso was born in Bagheria (where he is buried). This master of Italian realism donated many works to his native city, which he never forgot, and which are on view in the **Gallery of Modern Art** in the eighteenth-century **Villa Cattolica**.

Villa Palagonia is the most famous of the villas of Bagheria, built in 1715 by the architect Tommaso Maria Napoli for Prince Ferdinando Gravina di Alliata in an elliptical form and with a play of staircases and balconies.

▼ The entrance to the Baroque Villa Palagonia.

◄▲ Close-ups of anthropomorphic figures decorating Villa Palagonia.

Goethe called it the *Villa of Monsters* on account of its grotesque decorations. The **Room of Mirrors** with its fine ceiling is splendid and immense. **Villa Valguarnera** dating to 1721 and also built by the imaginative architect Tommaso Maria Napoli is located at the center of a large park of citrus trees. The front and back are embellished with sculpture by Ignazio Marabitti. One facade is concave at the center with two scenic staircases, while the other one faces the sea that can be seen from its many windows. **Villa Butera** was the first villa built in Bagheria in 1658, by Prince Giuseppe Branciforte, and also has a double staircase and is embellished with cupids.

▼ Villa Valguarnera in Bagheria.

■ Solunto

Solunto is one of the most important Greco-Roman archaeological sites in the province of Palermo, in an extraordinary location at the foot of the promontory of Mount Catalfano facing the sea. The Punic *Kafara* was founded in the fourth century BC and was destroyed in 397 BC by Dionysius of Syracuse to become the Greek *Solus* or *Soleis*. The Romans who occupied it in 254 BC called it *Solunto*, then in the ninth century the Arabs razed it to the ground.

◄ Statue uncovered during excavation works (Antiquarium).

The **Antiquarium** on site has on exhibit artifacts recovered from the excavations begun in 1826 and still in course, as well as a plan of the ancient city.

Entry into the archaeological area is along the *decumanus*, still paved with red bricks and cut across by lanes where the shops and dwelling houses, each with a cistern for collecting rainwater, are clearly recognizable. Of particular note are the **House of Leda** with mosaics depicting *Leda and the swan*, and the building known as **Gymnasium**, a rich patrician dwelling with a peristyle of Doric columns and paintings on the walls. Not much remains of the fine **Theater** not far away, over the **Agorà**, although part of the *cavea* and the *tiers* on which up to a thousand two hundred spectators could sit can be identified. Next to the theater is a rectangular **bouleuterion** or odeon with a small circular *cavea* where the council held its assemblies.

▼ The archaeological site of Solunto.

■ Mondello

Ten kilometers from Palermo is Mondello, the most photographed bay in Sicily and appearing on more post cards than any other. It lies among the rocks of Mount Pellegrino and Mount Gallo with a kilometer and a half of beach with fine white sand, a transparent turquoise sea with shoals. Originally a fishing village with a tuna processing plant and marshes, it was then reclaimed and *art nouveau* hotels, small and large villas sprang up. Since the nineteenth century Mondello has been the beach for the aristocratic classes of Palermo, where they come to eat fish even in winter.

Since the *bell'époque* when the "*dolce vita*" stayed up all night dancing the new dances from across the sea it has been a favorite haunt of the great European families. All that remains as reminder of those glorious days, wiped out by World War I, is the *Kursaal*, the *Art Nouveau* bathing establishment at the center of the bay (now a luxury restaurant), built on piles over the water in 1913 by the architect Rodolfo Stualket, with two hundred and thirteen cabins, each with an opening that let the ladies go directly into the water.

▼ The splendid bay of Mondello.

■ Isola delle Femmine

Pliny the Younger was the only one to imagine that lovely young women lived on the reef of the Isola delle Femmine, from the Arab *fim*, which means mouth and which then for the Sicilians became *Isola di li fimmini*. Not much more than an uninhabited reef with a sixteenth-century lookout **Tower**, built to keep a watch for pirates, around three hundred meters separates the island from the coast. The island, with a perimeter of one kilometer, is now a **Nature Reserve** for migrant birds and with one hundred and forty-four species of plants ranging from bushes to halophytes such as the delicate marine bird's foot trefoil.

▲ Isola delle Femmine.

A picturesque hamlet of fishermen and a famous beach resort, also known as Isola delle Femmine, lies on the stretch of coast facing the island. The **Chiesa Madre** is dedicated to Saint Salvatore. There is an old tuna processing plant, a fine well-equipped beach, a clear blue sea with coral shoals and restaurants serving fish and traditional cuisine. It is frequented even in winter by the Palermitani who come here, as they do to the nearby delightful marine hamlet of **SFERRACAVALLO** with its small harbor, to eat *spaghetti con le neonate*, tiny baby sardines that can only be fished from December to April.

▲▼ The seaside hamlet of Sferracavallo and a panorama of Capaci.

Capaci

Capaci is a pleasant seaside resort in the gulf of Carini, near the Palermo airport of Punta Raisia, with bare rock mountains rising up behind and with a well-equipped beach of fine white pebbles. But for the Italians the name is anything but joyous for in the early 1990s a

Mafia attack killed Judge Giovanni Falcone, his wife and his escorts, blowing up the car and wiping out one of Italy's best men. There is a monument here in their memory. Capaci arose around 1523 at the foot of the Santa Rosalia Montagnola and the fine **Cathedral** with an octagonal ground plan was begun then. It

▲► The Castle of Carini and the story of the hapless Baroness painted on a Sicilian cart.

has a double staircase on the Baroque facade and has frescoes by Giuseppe Tresca inside. Several **necropoli** not far from the Cathedral merit a visit.

■ Carini

The Sicani founded *Hyccara* in the tenth century BC. It was destroyed by the Greeks of Nicia in 414 BC and is now Carini, a town of twenty-five thousand inhabitants, ten kilometers from the sea, rebuilt by the Arabs on the slopes of the hill overlooking the citrus groves on the plain. Carini is synonymous with the **castle** that was built between the end of the eleventh and the beginning of the twelfth century, with its story of blood, passion and death. It was here that the beautiful Laura Lanza di Trabia, Baroness of Carini, was killed by her father, defending the honor of the family and of her husband after he had surprised her with her lover Ludovico Vernagallo. Many versions of the story have appeared since 1563, including a poem in the Sicilian dialect, and it has also become part of the repertory of the *puppet theater*.

The **castle** was built in Norman times and frequently altered in the course of the centuries by the various lords who lived here, the Chiaramonte, Moncada, La Grua. In a mixture of styles, the manor-house has a small *chapel* and *rooms* with wooden ceilings. Carini also has a fine eighteenth-century **Cathedral** or **Chiesa Madre** with a loggia on the facade and two flanking bell-towers. The interior is all frescoes and stuccos.

■ Terrasini

Once a fishing hamlet, Terrasini is now a lively seaside resort, with brightly colored houses, a small harbor, a clear turquoise sea, fine sandy beaches and white-veined red rocks, as at **Cala Rossa**, the enchanting bay named after its red rocks. There are discothèques and bars along the waterfront where one can eat at practically all hours of the night, waiting for the dawn.

The **Civic Museum** is housed in the fine *Palazzo Daumale*. In addition to palaeontological and ornithological collections and a collection of picturesque Sicilian carts, archaeological finds from the shoals of Terrasini are on display: Phoenician amphoras, Greek vases and Arab crafts of the tenth century.

■ Island of Ustica

Ustum, burned, is what the Romans called this island of black lava rocks that emerged from sea after a volcanic explosion. Ustica is the tortoise-shaped island in the middle of the Mediterranean with a pinch of the exotic, and is known for its lentils, small, black and soft. It is two hours from Palermo by ferry.

For those who love the sea and the sun, Ustica is paradise on earth, an uncontaminated wild island in a landscape of Mediterranean *mac-chia*, with crystal clear waters in al shades of blue, its shoals crowded with brightly colored forests of gorgonians, vast prairies of poseidonia seaweed, corals, sponges and countless types of fish swimming around among the wrecks of Roman ships and other archaeological finds. The Region of Sicily has instituted the first **Natural Marine Park** to safeguard this immense wealth.

The rocks falling sheer to the sea with euphorbia flowers in the crevices, conceal **grottoes** of extraordinary beauty, such as the **Blue Grotto** which takes its name from the color of the water, or the **Grotta della Pastizza**, or **Punta Galera** or of the **Spalmatore** with an adjacent small beach of white pebbles and low shoals, while the **Scoglio del Medico** rises solitary from the water, a favorite with scuba divers because of its many underwater cavities.

Falling sheer to the sea is *Capo Falconiera* with the ruins of the ma stodonic **Saracen Castle** overlook

► The lovely sea of Terrasini.

▲ ► The transparent waters of Punta Arpa and the splendid shoals of Ustica.

ing the town of Ustica and a favorite site for bird watchers looking for resident and migratory birds.

The vestiges of **prehistoric villages** and Phoenician and Carthaginian **necropoli** are at *Omo Morto* and *Colombaia*. Ustica has two hotels, but there are any number of small restaurants serving the local cuisine of fresh fish and lentils. Frivolity and noise are out, but at sunset it is a rite to sip an aperitif with swordfish patties at the *Bar Centrale* in the small square off limits to cars.

TRAPANI

▲▶ Trapani seen from Mount Erice and the Shrine of the Annunziata.

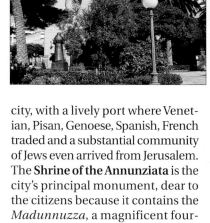

The city stretches out into the sea on a narrow sickle-shaped promontory. The Greeks called it *Drepanon* or sickle since legend has it that Trapani was formed by the sickle the goddess Demeter dropped as she was desperately looking for her daughter Persephone. Trapani (seven thousand inhabitants), opposite the Egadi Islands, is the most African part of Sicily, where the Arab influence is strongest. It was in this western corner of Sicily that the Elimi, the Phoenicians, Greeks, Carthaginians and Romans, Arabs and Normans dominated and left indelible marks, not only on the land but in the character of the people: an inertia, Arab fatalism and sensuality, together with a Phoenician entrepreneurial talent.

In the ninth century under the Arabs Trapani became a rich mercantile city, with a lively port where Venetian, Pisan, Genoese, Spanish, French traded and a substantial community of Jews even arrived from Jerusalem. The **Shrine of the Annunziata** is the city's principal monument, dear to the citizens because it contains the *Madunnuzza*, a magnificent fourteenth-century statue of a smiling *Madonna and Child*, by the Tuscan

◄▲ The dome of the Cathedral
and the *Coral Lamp*
by Fra' Matteo Baviera
(Pepoli Regional Museum).

Andrea Pisano, thought to be miraculous. The Church was built by the Carmelites between 1315 and 1332 and then renovated in 1770. The original fourteenth-century facade has a rose window and a Gothic portal. The rooms of the former convent house the **Pepoli Regional Museum** with precious collections of silver and gold work and objects in coral as well as

▼ The Ligny Tower, premises of the Museum of Prehistory and of the Sea.

▲ ▶ Wooden statues
of the *Mysteries* and the spiral
staircase of the bell tower
of the Church of San Domenico.

archaeological finds, paintings and statues. Every Christmas the museum organizes an exhibition of crèches, esteemed and requested throughout the world.

The **Cathedral of San Lorenzo** with its lovely green majolica domes was built in 1635 on the site of an older church and the Loggia of the Genoese. It was then enlarged and restructured by the architects Bonaventura Certo and Giovanni Biagio Amico. The Latin-cross interior with Baroque decorations contains various works of art including a splendid *Crucifixion* attributed to Van Dyck.

The seventeenth-century **Church of the Purgatory** keeps watch over the twenty wooden statues of the "Mysteries" dating to the seventeenth-eighteenth century and carried in the procession of the Passion of Christ during Holy Week. The **Church of San Domenico** is also a Baroque renovation but it still has its rose window, some frescoes inside and the apse where the *sarcophagus of Manfred*, son of Frederick III of Aragon, stands. The spiral staircase leading to the top of the bell tower is particularly scenic.

Province of Trapani

■ Erice

Erice, the ancient Eryx, is an enchanting medieval hamlet in stone, with small squares, courtyards and narrow paved passageways, perched on Mount San Giuliano and overlooking Trapani and the sea. The mythical origins relate that the king of the Elimi built a temple on the mountain to his mother, Venus. At night a bonfire was lit in the temple precincts and the temple and the mountain became a point of reference for sailors. Erice became a sacred city and the cult of Venus Erycina spread throughout the Mediterranean. For long fought over between the Phoenicians and Greeks, the city was Carthaginian up to 260 BC, till the Romans conquered it in 244 BC.

Since 1963, when the *Ettore Majorana Center for Culture and Science* was instituted in the former **Mona-stery of San Pietro**, Erice has become a citadel of science, known throughout the world and frequented by scholars as well as tourists who treasure this lovely city, known as the Italian Switzerland, but also appreciate the traditional almond paste sweets and the fabulous brightly colored rag rugs, made with the old technique of the *frazzata*, recycled strips of cloth woven in geometric patterns.

Erice is triangular in plan, with three city gates: **Trapani, Porta Spada** and **Porta Carmine**, and is surrounded by the monumental **Walls** built by the Elimi around the eighth century BC on which Phoenician inscriptions can be seen. The **Chiesa Madre** built in 1314 by Frederick II of Aragon is dedicated to Our Lady of the Assumption. The facade is preceded by a massive fifteenth-century porch and there are frescoes of Catalan school and works by Domenico Gagini inside. Next to it is a solitary two-sto-

▼ Panorama of Erice.

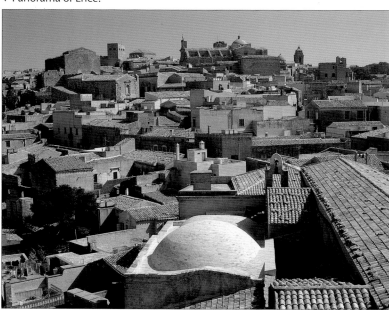

ried bell tower with Gothic two-light openings. The Norman **Churches of San Martino** and **San Giuliano** have been renovated and the second is today the premises of a cultural center. Fourteenth-century frescoes and sculpture by the Gagini are in the **Church of San Giovanni Battista**. The **Castle of Venus** rebuilt by the Normans stands on the site of the acropolis. Inside there are vestiges of columns, a sacred well, the remains of a Carthaginian house and Roman

baths. Nearby, surrounded by a flourishing garden, is **Castello Pepoli** with its famous **Torre del Balio**, emblem of Erice, once the governor's headquarters and from which there is a marvelous panorama of the sea, Valderice and the Egadi Islands.

▼ ► The Cathedral of Erice and view of the nave.

◀ Mosaic floor of the House of the Mosaics.

■ Mozia, Island of

Founded by the Phoenicians of Tyre in the eighth century BC, its Phoenician name Motya is said to mean *spinnery*. This fascinating silent and luxuriant little island, its forty hectares floating in the sea of the Laguna dello Stagnone in a landscape of white saltpans and windmills, is joined to the mainland by a causeway covered with water. Through the centuries the sand protected its spell-binding archaeology, surrounded by vineyards, olive groves, and prickly pears. Under the Phoenicians it became one of the most prosperous trading centers in the Mediterranean for the processing and dying of textiles. In 397 BC this highly strategic site was forced to surrender to the tyrant of Syracuse, Dionysius the Elder. The Carthaginians later reconquered the island. It was Joseph Whitaker, a wealthy English merchant, who rediscovered Mozia. He bought the island in the early twentieth century and began an excavation campaign which brought to light extraordinary masterpieces: ten thousand objects ranging from sculpture, vases, censers, jewels to mother goddesses are now on view in the **Whitaker Museum**, including the elegant sensual **Ephebus of**

▶ The elegant and sensuous *Ephebus of Motya*, symbol of the meeting of Punic and Greek civilizations.

Motya, a fifth-century BC armless marble statue of a youth.

The **House of the Amphorae** and the **House of the Mosaics** are what remain of two dwellings, their names obviously referring to the many amphorae found in the first, and the mosaic floor in black and white pebbles depicting *fighting animals* in the peristyle of the latter.

Next to the city of the dead, the **Archaic Necropolis** used for archaic cremation burials, is one of the most fascinating monuments, the **Tophet** or open-air sanctuary where human sacrifices were offered to the god Baal

▲▼ The Tophet, holy sanctuary where children were sacrificed, and the Cothon, Punic careenage basin, the only one of its kind in Sicily.

Hammon and Tanit and later to the Carthaginian Astarte. A small temple inside has stelae, funeral cippi and urns containing the remains of children scattered here and there. Near the **South Gate** is the **Cothon**, an artificial careenage basin measuring 50 by 37 meters, where the Semites repaired their damaged ships, identical with the one found in Carthage.

■ Marsala

Marsala, the Phoenician *Lily-baeum* founded by refugees from Motya in 397 BC, stands on the promontory of Cape Boeo, the farthest point of Western Sicily. With the Arabs in the ninth century the city took the name of *Mars-Alì*, port of Alì and it was from the port that the Saracens drew their greatest wealth. The name Marsala, like its history and landscape, brings to mind its excellent and famous wine, the first *Italian doc*, almost a liqueur the color of amber, known as Marsala. Its fame and fortune began with John Woodhouse, an English merchant from Liverpool, who first introduced it to his fellow countrymen. Giuseppe Garibaldi, the hero of the Risorgimento, was particularly fond of it and after he landed here on May 11,

▼ The facade of the imposing Cathedral dedicated to Saint Thomas of Canterbury.

▲ ► Vineyards for the production of *Marsala* wine and barrels for aging.

1860 with his 'Thousand' to drive the Bourbons from Sicily, a variety of this wine was called *Garibaldi dolce* in his honor.

Piazza della Repubblica is the old heart of Marsala with two imposing buildings: the Cathedral and **Palazzo Senatorio**, known also as La Loggia, with an eighteenth-century clock tower. The **Cathedral,** begun in Norman times and dedicated to Saint Thomas of Canterbury, was heavily bombed in World War II. The facade is flanked by two small bell towers and decorated with sculpture, while inside, in addition to sculpture by the Gagini family, there is a *Presentation of Jesus in the Temple,* a sixteenth-century work by Mariano Riccio.

Behind the Cathedral, the **Tapestry Museum** contains eight splendid sixteenth-century Flemish tapestries, gift of Philip II of Spain to the bishop of the city, depicting the *War waged by Titus against the Jews.* The imposing **Complex of San Pietro** is in the old Jewish quarter of the Giudecca. This former sixteenth-century Benedictine convent is square in plan and has a tower known as **Specola**. The monastery now houses the **Museum of the Risorgimento**.

The small **Church of San Giovanni** with a fine sculpture of *Saint John* by Antonello Gagini is at Capo Boeo, facing the sea. It was built over a grotto with a well, the cave of the legendary Sibyl of Lilybaeum, priestess of Apollo who drew her prophesies from the transparency of the water.

The **Archaeological Museum** is inside the **Baglio Anselmi**, an old winery, and contains archaeological finds from Mozia and Marsala, as well as Punic and Roman necropoli. The

▲ Flemish tapestry in the Tapestry Museum.

wreck of a Punic ship, a *liburna* thirty-five meters long that sank on March 10, 241 BC in the Egadi Islands during the First Punic War with the Romans and was recovered by the underwater archaeologist Honor Frost in 1969, holds pride of place in the museum. The wreck is still being studied by experts, including NASA, for the construction techniques hold many secrets. Despite the centuries under water the nails have not rusted.

▼ The splendid *Dancing Satyr* dating to the fourth century BC

■ Mazara del Vallo

The Arab Mazara del Vallo from the Phoenician name meaning *castle* lies on the canal harbor of Sicily, on the estuary of the Mazaro River, with a fishing harbor that is one of the largest and best equipped in Italy and which supplies thirty per cent of the national catch.

In its architecture, agriculture, gardens, cuisine and town planning with its labyrinthine historical center like the *kasbah* of an Arab *medina*, its lanes and alleys, courtyards and small squares, Mazara is the Sicilian city that has most retained the culture and memory of Islam. The inhabitants move through the spice-scented streets dressed in long white kaftans and the women, in their brightly colored garments, are veiled and speak a language that is Arab-Sicilian.

It was with the Arabs, who landed at Capo Granitola in 827 to conquer Sicily, that Mazara – as narrated by Idrisi, the Arab geographer – attained its economic and cultural heyday and was at the head of the administrative

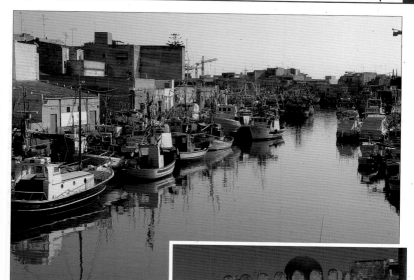

▲► The canal port and the Church of San Nicolò Regale that overlooks the canal.

district Val di Mazara. The Normans, who conquered it in 1073, built churches and monasteries and it was here that they called the first Parliament of Sicily.

Since 1998 Mazara del Vallo has been the city of the **Dancing Satyr** believed to be by Praxiteles, a bronze statue of a faun, a mythical figure who accompanied Dionysius, the god of wine, together with the maenads. Caught in a fishing net and restored in Rome, it is now the main tourist attraction of the city. Mazara has dedicated a museum to this beautiful daemon of Hellenistic Greece, dating to the fourth-third century BC, two and a half meters high, with his head and one leg thrown back, in the sixteenth-century deconsecrated **Church of Sant'Egidio** in Piazza Plebiscito.

The historical quarters *San Giovanni*, *San Francesco*, *Xitta* and *Giudecca* in the *kasbah*, heart of the city, have some interesting churches such as the Baroque **Church and Monastery of Santa Veneranda,** with two tiers and two bell loggias with a Rococo portal covered with carving and friezes, the eleventh-century **Church of San Michele**, rebuilt in the seventeenth century, the **Seminary of the Chierici** with its double loggia, and the **Church**

▶ A lane in the *kasbah* of the historical center.

of San Nicolò Regale, in the San Giovanni quarter overlooking the harbor. This is a Norman gem of 1124, Greek cross on a square ground plan, with a charming pink dome.

The **Cathedral** was built around 1088 and then remodeled in the seventeenth and nineteenth centuries. The apse and walls are original. Over the portal on the facade is a sixteenth-century bas-relief of *Roger on horseback trampling a Moor*. The interior is a profusion of gold and stuccoes, a real museum with Hellenistic sarcophagi and other works. Of particular note are the sixteenth-century *Transfiguration*, a marble group of six statues by Antonello and Antonino Gagini in the apse, and the *Stories of* *Saint Egidio* in the marble portal by Bartolomeo Berrettaro. The *Chris Pantokrator*, a thirteenth-century fresco, is splendid and almost hidden in an ogee niche near the transept

◀▼ Bas-relief on the portal of the Cathedral with *Roger on horseback trampling a Moor* and panorama of the roofs of Mazara del Vallo.

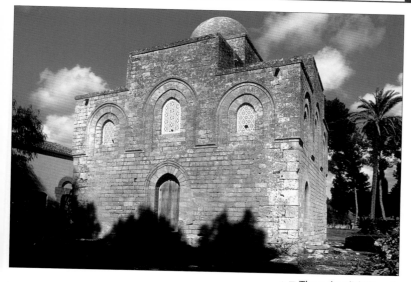

▲ ▼ The splendid Church of the Trinità in Delia and the vigorous fifth-century BC *Ephebus of Selinunte* (Municipal Museum of Castelvetrano).

■ Castelvetrano

Castelvetrano with thirty thousand inhabitants in the valleys of the Belice and Delia Rivers is the city famous for its black bread, oil, wine and furniture. The ancient Sicana *Legum* came to be known as *Castrum veteranum*. After the Arab domination, in 1299 it was the feud of the Tagliavia barons and then a principate of the Pignatelli family.

Overlooking *Piazza Don Carlo d'Aragona*, heart of the historical center, are the **Church of the Purgatorio** (1642), **Palazzo Pignatelli** (13th cent.), restored several times, and the **Chiesa Madre** (16th cent.) with a finely carved stone portal. The interior is frescoed with stuccoes (particularly fine those by Serpotta between the choir and the presbytery), the lovely *Saint Theresa of Avila with the Madonna and Saint Joseph*, attributed to Guglielmo Borremans. The **Municipal Museum**, in addition to the archaeological finds

from Selinunte (the *Lead Lamina* with a fifth-century BC *lex sacra* inscribed, recently returned to the city by the Getty Museum) has the lovely **Ephebus of Selinunte**, a bronze statue of a youth 85 centimeters high, dating to circa 470 BC, stolen in 1962 but later found. The art historian Cesare Brandi called this superb example of the passage of archaic to classic art, with a subtle treatment of the forms, one of the twenty finest Italian masterpieces. In the nearby **DELIA**, only three and a half kilometers away, the lovely **Church of the Santissima Trinità** merits a visit. It is a Norman structure on an Orthodox-Byzantine square ground plan with three apses and with a dome and incorporates Arab influences.

■ Selinunte

The mutilated temples of Selinus or Selinunte overlooking the sea on the beach of Marinella are the color of gold and at sunset gleam in the last lights of the sun. The splendid archaeological site is a labyrinth of endless stone ruins scattered over two hundred and fifty hectares. Wild flowers and parsley make this scenic landscape, a tragic reminder of the brutality and inhumanity of history, somewhat less solemn and funereal. Selinunte is one of the largest archaeological parks in Europe. Here the Greeks, who founded it in 628 BC, raised nine temples to their gods, among the most beautiful and perfect examples of Doric architecture decorated with metopes, the only ones of their kind in Sicily. The city took its name from the two rivers on either side, *Hipsa* and *Sélinus*, (now Cottone and Modione). *Sélinus* comes

▼► Temple E still has parts
of the entablature.

from the Greek name for wild parsey which still grows in the area.
In just two centuries the city attained its zenith. Virgil describes it as full of palms. It was the westernmost of the Greek cities and allied itself with the Carthaginians up to the battle of Himera when it became an ally of Syacuse. Always at odds with Segesta, allied with the Carthaginians for the dominion and enlarging of its borders, it was destroyed in 409 BC by the Carthaginian Hannibal. Sixteen

thousand Selinuntini were killed and five thousand were taken as slaves, after which the temples were sacked. Thus the story of Selinunte – according to the historians – ended in a massacre. An earthquake in the Middle Ages canceled what little remained. Ruins dating to the fifth century BC such as **Temples O, A** and **B**, the smallest probably dedicated to the Agrigento philosopher Empedocles, are on the **Acropolis** that drops down to the sea. **Temple C** however dates to

▲ ◄ Temples C and D
and a fascinating picture
of Temple C with
a Punic mosaic in the foreground

the sixth century BC and is the oldest and one of the largest in Greek temple architecture. Only a few columns remain standing. Porticoed, it was a peripteral hexastyle temple, measuring 64x24 meters, with 6 columns on the short sides and 17 on the long sides, and had a frieze of gorgon masks and the splendid metopes now in the Archaeological Museum in Palermo. *Tanit*, the Punic goddess, is depicted in the mosaic floor. Nearby are the ruins of

Temple D (sixth cent. BC), perhaps consecrated to Aphrodite, as well as the remains of later Punic dwellings (fourth-third cent. AD).

Temples E, F and **G** are on the **Eastern Hill**. **Temple E** (5th cent. BC), re-erected in 1957, displays the rational and harmonious tendency of the Greek mind in establishing a perfect relationship between buildings and landscape. Possibly consecrated to Hera protectress of marriage and births, the temple is hexastyle with 38 columns. Little remains of the smallest sixth century BC **Temple F** except for a few metopes depicting Athena and Dionysius. **Temple G** (6th cent. BC), dedicated to Apollo, protector of Selinunte, was particularly imposing: 6120 square meters, a peristyle of 4

► The ruins of the Sanctuary of the Malophoros.

columns, 16.27 meters high with a circumference of 10.7 *meters*. Only one of the columns has been raised, a tragic reminder of what has been lost.

Near the hill is what remains of the **Sanctuary of the Malophoros**, or *bearer of the pomegranate*, dedicated to Demeter, goddess of fertility. Numerous terracotta statuettes of female divinities have been found in the area and some are now in the Sicilian museums. A wall, the *teménos*, enclosed the sanctuary which consisted of a sacred building in the shape of a *Mycenaean mégaron*.

At **CAMPOBELLO DI MAZARA**, six kilometers from Selinunte, are the **Cave** or **Quarries of Cusa**. A surreal site, an immense park of column drums, blocks of stone, some rough hewn, others still attached to the rock, have been lying there for two thousand five hundred years surrounded by prickly pears and olive trees. It was in these quarries of calcareous tufa, called *Ramuxara* by the Arabs, that the fine-grained stone used in building the temples was extracted. It is calculated that the Greeks quarried around a hundred and fifty thousand cubic meters of stone to build the temples of Selinunte.

▼ Blocks of stone from the quarries of Cusa, used by the Selinuntines to build their temples.

■ Gibellina

The new Gibellina in the Valley of Belice can be thought of as an open air museum of contemporary art. It rose from the rubble of the earthquake of 1968 which razed it to the ground and generous architects and artists such as Burri, Pomodoro, Cascella, Cagli, Fontana, Schifano, Guttuso and others helped turn it into a cosmopolitan town.

The new town rose eighteen kilometers from the old. The spectacular **Cretto** by Alberto Burri, a flow of cement on the ruins of the old city, with a labyrinth of cracks, is the symbol of the reconstruction of Gibellina. The imposing **City Gate** made by Pietro Consagra in 1980 is in the form of a star. The artist, who recently died, also rebuilt the gates of the cemetery, while what remains of the Baroque **Palazzo Di Lorenzo** has been annexed to the **Cultural Center** designed by the architects Vittorio Gregotti, Giuseppe Samonà and Giuseppe Pirroni. The **Museum of Contemporary Art** contains numerous works donated to Gibellina by the artists, including some by the great Sicilian painter Renato Guttuso.

■ Calatafimi

On May 15, 1860 – the year Italy was unified – Calatafimi was the theater of the victory of Garibaldi's troops, with the aid of the *picciotti*, or local young men, over the Bourbon army. On the Pianto Romano hill an **Ossuary-Monument** was built in memory by the artist Ernesto Basile. Calatafimi-Segesta, its present name, is a town of eight thousand inhabi-

◀▼ The Mendini tower and Alberto Burri's *Cretto* in Gibellina.

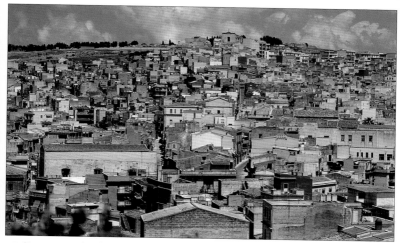

▲▼ Panorama of Calatafimi and Ossuary-Memorial Monument at Pianto Romano.

tants surrounded by pines and cork groves. It was built by the Arab-Berbers, on the slopes of two hills, around the Byzantine **Castle of Sant'Eufemio**. Thereafter it was a land of feuds, first with the Counts of Modica and then others, but the city grew with the arrival of the mendicant orders. It was destroyed in 1968 by a violent earthquake. *The Festival of the Holy Crucifix* is celebrated in Calatafimi in memory of miraculous events related to the crucifix dating to 1657. The imposing celebration, a mixture of faith and folklore, takes place every five years at the beginning of May with processions and allegorical floats that illustrate episodes from the Bible. Calatafimi has three lovely churches: the **Church of Santa Caterina,** the **Church of San Michele** and the **Chiesa Madre**. The first is Baroque and was designed by the priest-architect Giovanni Biagio Amico. It contains a triptych with a *Madonna and Saints* from the shrine of the Madonna of Giubino. The second contains a sixteenth-century *holy water font* and a fifteenth-century *wooden Crucifix*. The Chiesa Madre, twelfth century but renovated in the sixteenth, has a *Madonna with Saints*, a marble group by Bartolomeo Berrettaro, in the apse.

■ Segesta

A theater and a temple, two majestic buildings on the bare hill of Monte Barbaro, are all that remain of Segesta, a dead city. It was founded by the Elimi, a mythical people who according to Thucydides were descended from the Trojans.

Segesta took its name from a Trojan nymph who cared for Aeneas when he landed in Sicily. Ambitious Segesta in the fifth century BC was at the apex of its wealth and power and permeated with Greek customs and culture, but always bickering over boundaries with its rival Selinunte, ally of Syracuse. Segesta, ally of the Carthaginians, was destroyed at the end of the fourth century BC by the tyrant of Syracuse Agathocles who could not tolerate – says Diodorus Siculus – the shame of having asked the Carthaginians for aid. Afterwards with the Romans, in virtue of their affinity and relationship with the Elimi, Segesta once more became a city *"libera et immunis"*. The extraordinary Doric **Temple** that domi-

▲◄ The solitary Temple and the Theater of Segesta.

nates the harsh landscape and has been compared to the Parthenon is absolutely perfect. It was built outside the walls, between 430-420 BC, and is a hexastyle peripteral temple, with 36 unfluted columns resting on a stepped stylobate and supporting a pediment and entablature with smooth metopes and triglyphs. There is no cella and the covering is missing.

The **Theater** built in the third century BC and facing north is a hemicycle sixty-four meters in diameter. It housed four thousand spectators in the **cavea** with twenty tiers dug into the rock, divided into seven sectors, while the **orchestra** with a diameter of eighteen meters concealed a secret passageway from which the actors could appear and surprise the public, while the **scena** had side wings.

Every two years, summer evenings, the old magic of the theater comes back to life with plays of ancient authors, sponsored by the Tourist Bureau of Trapani.

▲ ◄ Panorama of Alcamo and its vineyards.

◼ Alcamo

Alcamo with its forty-five thousand inhabitants is a hard working and dynamic town. In addition to agriculture (citrus and olive groves and vineyards) the economy is based on the working of the "hermits' stone" or travertine, as well as wood and wrought iron.

The city is famous as the birthplace of the thirteenth-century poet *Ciullo* or *Cielo d'Alcamo,* author of one of the earliest texts to be written in Italian "*Rosa Fresca Aulentissima*". It is also known for its excellent *Bianco*

d'Alcamo, a doc dry wine which was listed as an excellent wine back in 1549 by one of the Pope's oenologists. Since antiquity Alcamo has been the crossroads between Palermo and Trapani, in a valley of Monte Bonifato between two castles: Bonifato and Calatubo. The city takes its name from *Alqam* (muddy earth) or from *manzil Alqamah* (country house of Alqamah, the Arab founder) but the Muslims called it also *Rabbid Allah* (thanks to Allah) for the abundance of the land.

In 972 the Saracens first built the fortress country houses on Monte Bonifato to keep guard over the communication routes, then they embellished it with mosques, as two travelers, the geographer Idrisi and the Andalusian Ibn Jubair, tell us. Frederick II of Swabia in 1233 interned the Arabs of Alcamo after they revolted and the remaining inhabitants went down into the valley. As feudal land it was dominated by the Peralta, Ventimiglia and Chiaramonte families.

► ▼ The lovely dome of the Chiesa Madre of Alcamo and the Gothic-Swabian Castel of the Counts of Modica.

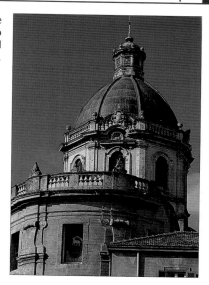

Some of the churches are worth visiting. The lovely **Chiesa Madre** dedicated to Our Lady of the Assumption is a seventeenth-century adaptation of an earlier fourteenth-century church by the architects Angelo Italia and Giuseppe Diamanti. The inside is covered with frescoes by the Flemish artist Guglielmo Borremans and sculpture by the school of Gagini while the *Crucifix* in the second chapel on the right and the *Death of the Virgin* in the left chapel are by Antonello Gagini. The eighteenth-century **Church of Santa Oliva** by Giovanni Battista Amico which overlooks *Piazza Ciullo*, formerly Piano Maggiore, historical center of the city, contains the *Statue of Saint Oliva*, a masterpiece by Antonello Gagini, and a painting by Pietro Novelli, the *Release of the Souls from Purgatory*, on the high altar. A *Saint Theresa* and an *Annunciation* in the **Badia Grande** or **Church of San Salvatore** of the fifteenth-century Benedictine monastery are by the same painter.

With its imposing mass the Gothic-Swabian **Castle of the Counts of Modica** dominates *Piazza della Repubblica*. It was built by the Chiaramonte brothers in 1350 on a rhomboidal plan with four towers, two cylindrical and two square, while the Arab castle of **Calatubo**, on a rocky spur, is now abandoned.

▲ Panorama
of Castellammare del Golfo.

■ Castellammare del Golfo

Castellammare del Golfo is named after the splendid gulf that stretches from Capo Rama to San Vito Lo Capo. The town is embedded in its bay, at the foot of a mountain and slopes softly down to the sea, up to the small peninsula of white beaches. It is dominated by the imposing Arab **Castle** with its cylindrical towers with the white houses of fishermen all around. Restored by the Normans and the Swabians, the castle is one of the most interesting fortresses in Western Sicily. Castellammare del Golfo was the emporium of Segesta, what the Arabs called *Al Madarig*, the steps, with a steep descent. Today it is also a popular seaside resort.

To visit are: the **Chiesa Madre** with its elegant facade, an eighteenth-century reconstruction by the architect Giuseppe Mariani, and the splendid **Small Church of the Rosario**, known also as of the *Madonna di l'agnuni* with a bas-relief of a *Madonna and Child, Saint* and a *Crucifix* over the portal.

■ Scopello

This seaside resort near San Vito Lo Capo is only seven kilometers away, and can also be reached on foot through the extraordinary **Zingaro Nature Reserve**, seven kilometers of protected flora and fauna where rocks falling sheer to the sea give way to beaches and bays.
Scopello, whose name comes from

◄ Prickly pear, growing
in the Zingaro Nature Reserve.

▲► The tuna fishery
of Piano Battaglia at Scopello
and a seafood couscous,
typical dish of San Vito lo Capo.

the Greek or Latin *skopelos-scopellum* meaning reef-cliff with reference to the imposing *faraglioni* or vertical reefs in this stretch of the coast, is in the region the Greeks called *Cetaria* because of the abundance of tuna fish in its waters. The Arabs rechristened it *Iscubul Iakut* and enlarged the tuna port by building the **Baglio**, from the Arab *bahal*, courtyard, around which the picturesque hamlet of Scopello developed. Emperor Frederick II in 1220 gave it as feud to a colony of emigrant Piacentini.

The tuna fishery closed down in the nineteen eighties and is now a **Museum** where the objects and equipment used in capturing the tuna fish are on exhibit.

■ San Vito Lo Capo

This marine hamlet of white square houses is located on a bay of fine white sand, between Capo San Vito and Punta di Solante. Caressed by a blue sea, this well-known seaside resort developed around the Saracen fort that was transformed in the thirteenth century into the **Shrine of San Vito**. The saint, after whom the hamlet is named, had taken refuge in the area with his nurse Crescenzia who also became a saint for she fled from Diocletian's persecutions. San Vito Lo Capo became internationally known in 1998 for its *Cous Cous Fest*, a festival that lasts seven days, with odors, colors, flavors, music and people of every race and religion, in which the best cooks vie with each other in preparing the best couscous. This dish with so much history and myth now expresses ecumenism and brotherhood between the West and the Near East.

◀▲ View of Favignana
and capturing tuna fish
during the *mattanza*.

■ Egadi Islands

Favignana, Marettimo, Levanzo, Maraone, the reef of Porcelli and the tiny isle of Formica form the archipelago of the Egades facing Trapani, three pearls on the sea where the Tyrrhenian mixes with the Mediterranean which Homer called *Aegusa*, *Hiera* and *Phorbantia*. In summer they are frequented by a special type of tourist, one who loves wild nature, silence, the sea, rides on mule back, the genuine local cuisine. A **Marine Reserve** has been set up in the Egadi Islands, lived in for the most part by fishermen. The reserve consists of 523 sq. km. and preserves the virgin shoals with their wealth of flora and fauna, archaeology and history – since it was in these waters that the First Punic War ended in 241 BC after the battle between Hamilcar Barca's Carthaginians and the Romans

led by Lutatius Catulus – and amphoras, wrecks and sculpture still rest on the shoals, sometimes washed up by the sea.

FAVIGNANA was Homer's *Aegades* the island of goats, where Ulysses landed. Butterfly shaped with Mount Santa Caterina at the center, it is the largest island in the archipelago and its destiny and history are connected to the Florio family, the lords of the island, to the tuna fish, to the tuna factory, to the tuna kill, which in May and June still repeats the cruel spectacle, the rite, of the *mattanza*. The first cans of tuna fish in oil came from the **Florio tuna fishery**, a splendid example of industrial architecture. The coasts are one cove after the other, with grottoes, sinuous recesses and bays, such as **Cala San Nicola** with the cave in which Phoenician Punic inscriptions were found, while remains of Roman times were found on the **Bagno delle donne** site, or like **Cala Azzurra**, with its beach of Burrone and then **Cala Rotonda** and the

▲▼ The hamlet of Levanzo with its small harbor and a view of Marettimo.

loveliest **Cala Rossa,** amphitheater shaped and so-called for the blood the Carthaginians shed when defeated by the Romans in the Punic war. Opposite are the **Cave di Tufo** or Tufa Quarries washed by the transparent turquoise sea, a paradise for tourists who meet evenings in the piazza of the town on the small harbor. **LEVANZO** is the island opposite Favignana. Rock paintings of tunas, human figures and hunting scenes in the **Grotto of the Genovese** bear witness to the fact that it was inhabited in prehistoric times. Levanzo is the smallest of the Egadi Islands, rather bare it serves as pasture for goats and sheep and is the haunt of migratory birds. There are also places to swim in absolute silence such as **Cala Tramontano** and **Cala Minnola,** two small beaches in the midst of rocks

▶ Peninsula of Punta Troia at Marettimo with the Castle of Arab origins.

falling sheer to the sea. The latter, surrounded by pines and facing the faraglioni, is particularly enchanting.

MARETTIMO is the furthest and most unsullied island, morphologically quite different with mountains and hot water springs gushing from the cracks of the many grottoes. It is a hamlet of square white houses, with blue windows, all right on the bay. For the Greeks it was *Hiera*, the sacred, and Marettimo really does have something mystic about it, a paradise where time has stopped in the midst of a blue ocean, fragrant with rosemary and thyme, the aromatic herbs from which it takes its name (seathyme). Its enchanted places can be discovered on muleback, on foot or by sea, with the surprising **Grotte del Cammello** where one seems to be in a swimming pool or **del Presepe**, with its stalactites and stalagmites that look like statues and that change color depending on the light of the sun.

■ Island of Pantelleria

The color of its rocks and extinct volcanoes make Pantelleria the black pearl of the Mediterranean. It is closer to Tunisia than to Italy and the winds roam free, which is why it was called *Bent el Rhia* – daughter of the wind – by the Arabs.

▼ The Elephant Arch, a rock sculpture and symbol of Pantelleria.

▲▶ Specchio di Venere, a lake of sulfur water in a crater and a Sese, a Sesiote funerary monument in Pantelleria.

Pantelleria is the island of ca-pers, of the zibibbo grape from which the famous *Passito* and *Moscato di Pantelleria* wines are made. It is a harsh, wild and un-contaminated island, where night life is non-existent and vacations are of a Spartan type. There are hardly any beaches on Pantelleria and ac-cess to the sea is not always easy, the African sun is scorching and the wind brings relief, the sea is transparent and blue with shoals rich in ma-rine flora and fauna, some of which tropical, such as the pearl cyster.
It is a magical island, with an ori-ental atmosphere, where the influ-ence and mark of the Arabs who lived here for four hundred years are strong: in *the stone gardens* that protect plants and cultures from the wind, in the names of the towns, in the gastron-omy and flavors, in the dwellings and *dammusi*, the typical squared stone houses with white domes. It is a fa-vorite with VIPs and many have

bought *dammusi* and turned them into palatial dwellings, as well as mak-ing passito wine.
Pantelleria, the largest of the Sicil-ian islands, is also known for its *fava-re*, hot sulfur jets spurting from cracks in the rocks, such as **Specchio di Ve-nere**, a lake of sulfur water, at **Cala Denti**, encircled by pointed reefs near **Cala Levante**, the bay dominated by the elephant arch, a natural rock sculp-ture, the most photographed em-blem of the island.
Three thousand years before Christ the island was inhabited by the Se-siotes, a people who extracted ob-sidian, a black vitreous stone, which they traded in the Mediterranean. The **Sesi**, hemispherical funeral monu-ments in stone with cells inside where the bodies were laid in fetal position, bear witness to their presence.

AGRIGENTO

Agrigento, the Greek *Akragas*, the Roman *Agrigentum*, is reached via the arid Akragas viaduct, all uphill, and so high it makes one dizzy.

The opulent hedonistic ancient Agrigento which Pindar called "the loveliest inhabited city among mortals", lies in the millenary Valley of the Temples. The city of today is perched at the top of the *Girgenti* and *Atenea* hills, attached to an unchanging past as it moves on into modern times. The tourist who comes here is often in a hurry and building speculation has been rife. Yet certain corners of the historical center still have an Arab imprint, with charming buildings and the town plan, the names of squares and stairways, and above all the slow tempo of life, with a sense of fatalism and resignation, in the dark burning eyes of the curly-headed dark-skinned natives.

Agrigento was the birthplace of the philosopher Empedocles (and more recently of authors such as Luigi Pirandello, Leonardo Sciascia and An-

drea Camilleri). Mother of the great Greco-Siciliote civilization, it was founded in 581 BC by Greek colonists from Gela, between Gela and Selinunte and the Akragas and Hipsas Rivers (now Sant'Anna and San Biagio). The city attained its golden age in the years 488-427 BC under the tyrant Theron, lover of the beautiful, of letters and art, and it was destroyed by the Carthaginians in 406 BC. Empedocles said that the Agrigentini built as if they were to live in eternity and that they lived in the pleasures and luxury as if they were to die the following day.

The city became Roman in 210 BC and was later occupied by the Byzantines. In 827 under Arab rule the city of *Kirkent* then *Girgenti* flourished once more, second only to Palermo and seat of the emirate. It was then that Agrigento abandoned the valley for the top of the hills. After the Norman conquest the city became

▼ The original two-light openings of the Monastery of Santo Spirito.

▲ The old Cathedral of Agrigento.

a diocese and churches, convents and monasteries were built.

The most elegant street in the city is *Via Atenea*, which takes on life every evening in the *struscio* or promenade, with *boutiques*, stands and shops, interrupted by lanes, stairways and flowering courtyards, leading to the building the Agrigentini hold dear, the **Monastery of Santo Spirito** or **Badia**. It was built in the thirteenth century by Marchisia Prefoglio for the Benedictine nuns who still live there. They are famous for the marzipan sweets they make and a special sweet *couscous* with pistachios and candied fruit. The **Church** has undergone alterations but still has its lovely *Gothic portal* and rose window on the facade. The interior is decorated with stuccoes by Giacomo Serpotta. There is a lovely fountain in the small **cloister**, and the two-light openings on the side framing the door of the **Chapter Hall** are original.

The **Church of Santa Maria dei Greci** with its luxuriant palm garden dates to the eleventh century, and was built on the vestiges of a Doric temple dedicated to the goddess Athena (a few remains are still visible). The Greek-rite church contains Byzantine frescoes, in part faded.

The Cathedral is the tallest building in Agrigento, erected around the year thousand by Bishop Gerlando. Preceded by a staircase and flanked by a fifteenth-century bell tower with blind one-light openings and a balcony, the three-aisled interior has a profusion of frescoes and Baroque stuccoes. From the presbytery one can hear, thanks to the echo, what is whispered at the entrance to the Cathedral.

An embalmed body in a suit of armor is in the right aisle. For the Church these are the mortal remains of Saint Felix, while for the Agrigentini they belong to the famous Christian paladin Brandimarte – sung by the poet Ludovico Ariosto – killed by the Arabs and buried in the church as Orlando wished. The splendid *Madonna and Child* attributed to Guido Reni is in the **Sacristy** and the **archive** holds the *Letter to the devil*, a singular and curious apocryphal seventeenth-century missive sent to Sister Maria Crocifissa Tomasi to lead her into temptation.

■ Valley of the Temples

It is in this Valley that the Greeks celebrated their gods and after twenty-five centuries the visitor who pauses here, overwhelmed by the power of the site, still feels their presence.

The magnificent temples here were almost all built in the fifth century BC, marvelously close to each other and overlooking the sea. They are surrounded by age-old almond and olive trees, accoompanied by the deafening song of the cicadas, and the intense blinding light reflected in the golden sandstone. This is one of the great places of the spirit.

The entire Valley is one of the finest archaeological sites in Sicily and has been declared a World Heritage Site by UNESCO.

Every year in February, Agrigento celebrates the Almond Blossom Festival among its temples, a propitiatory rite for the arrival of spring, with

▼ The Temple of Hera Lacinia.

roots in Greek myth, the love of the Achaean Acamante and Fillide.

Rising up solitary, on the highest point of the hill, is the **Temple of Hera Lacinia** (the Roman Juno, wife of Zeus), goddess of fertility and patron of marriage. Built between 450-440 BC, preceded by a sacred altar, it consisted of three areas: the *opisthodomos*, the *cella* with the statue of the goddess, and the *pronaos*. Only 25 of the original 34 columns, 6 at each end and 13 along the sides, are still standing, some with their architrave. Destroyed by the Carthaginians, it was restored by the Romans. Then in the Middle Ages an earthquake left it as you see it today.

It was here that the Greeks celebrated marriages, but the temple was above all the shrine where women came to ask the goddess for her favors.

The majestic **Temple of Concord** is one of the loveliest in its elegant Doric style, with the harmony and perfection of the greatness of the Greeks mixed with a sense of mystery still there after twenty-five centuries.

In ocher sandstone that turns golden at sunset, it was built in 430 BC. It is a peripteral hexastyle building with 6 columns on the front and back and 11 on the long sides, 6.75 meters high and resting on four steps, with a total area of 19.758 sq. m. From the cella two spiral staircases led to an attic space.

Originally covered in colored stucco, the name Concord came to light in a Latin inscription nearby. It has survived because it was transformed into a Christian basilica in 597.

▼ View of the Valley of Temples.

► The superb Temple of Concord.

The **Temple** dedicated to **Heracles** dates to the sixth century BC. It was here that the Agrigentini celebrated their sacred festivals, the *Eraclee*, and it was here that his bronze statue was located. The temple had 38 columns, of which only 8 have been raised, 4 of which with capitals. The temple is visible from all parts of the valley. There is an early Christian **necropolis** beneath the road, with loculi dug into the rock walls in the *hypogea of Villa Aurea*, called *Catacombs of Fragapane*.

The **Tomb of Theron** in the western archaeological area is a Roman monument dating to the first century BC and not Greek as previously thought. Square in form, four Ionic columns with Doric capitals support the entablature.

The **Temple of the Olympian Zeus** was of majestic proportions. It was never finished but the tyrant Theron wanted it to be the largest in the Mediterranean. Now it is not much more than a ruin.

▲► The Temple of Heracles, sixth cent. BC, and the massive Tomb of Theron.

▲ Telamon, a gigantic male statue that supported the entablature of the Temple of the Olympian Zeus.

Begun in 480 BC, Carthaginian prisoners taken in the battle of Himera were employed in its construction. As described by Diodorus Siculus, the temple was 112 meters long and 56 wide, with columns 20 meters high and it covered an area of 6500 sq. m. The eight-meter high **Telamons** or Atlas figures that supported the entablature give an idea of how imposing it must have been.

The **Kolymbetra** are historical and suggestive gardens. Originally simply an immense basin five hectares in size created by Theron which was to supply the city with water, it was then transformed by the Arabs into flourishing gardens with rare plants, orchards and orange groves, with Saracen hypogea and cisterns.

The gardens were restored by the F.A.I. (Italian Fund for the Environment) and are now open to the public. They are near the monument that is the symbol of Agrigento, the fifth-century BC **Temple of the Dioscuri**, or of Castor and

◄ The old Gardens of the Kolymbetra.

Pollux, surrounded by age-old agaves and with 4 of its original 34 columns. The circular altar of the sixth-fifth century BC **Temple of Kore and Demeter** also stands in the same sacred area surrounded by the ruins of sacred buildings, moats and enclosures. The **Hellenistic-Roman quarter** of the third-fourth century AD stretches out over an area of 10,000 sq. m. with the remains of buildings, shops and patrician villas with mosaics.

The charming Romanesque-Gothic **Church of San Nicola** that overlooks the Valley of the Temples was built in 1200 by Cistercian monks. It has a nave only and four chapels, in the second of which is the *Sarcophagus of Phaedra*, a Roman marble, with decorations depicting the *myth of Hippolytus and Phaedra*. A curious fact is that many Agrigentini get married in this church.

The **Ekklesia**, next to the church, dates to the fourth century BC. Civic assemblies were held in this circular area with 22 tiers dug into the rock, divided into 5 wedge-shaped sectors. Next to it is the small **Temple of Falaride**, dating to Roman times.

The excellent **Regional Archaeological Museum** is in the former Cistercian convent. Second in Sicily in

▼ The Temple of the Dioscuri.

importance, and opened in 1967, it contains over 6000 finds in twenty rooms. These include vases, dinoi (sacrificial vases), kraters, Greek amphoras and terracotta figures and heads, such as that of a Kore and of male divinities, or the original *telamon* as well as Hellenistic sarcophagi and sculpture. The splendid sculpture of a youth, the **Ephebus of Agrigento** (fifth cent. BC), a virile nude kouros, was found in the cistern near the temple of Kore.

The house where Luigi Pirandello was born on June 28, 1867 is in the **CAOS** district in **Villaseta**, a few kilometers from Agrigento. Facing the sea, it is surrounded by a sun-baked landscape of age-old olive trees. Now a museum, it contains all the memorabilia of the Nobel prize author, one of the greatest of the twentieth century and considered the father of contemporary Italian theater, with works such as *Uno nessuno centomila, Sei personaggi in cerca d'autore (Six characters in search of an author), Pensaci Giacomino*. His ashes are immured in a "*rough stone*" below a withered pine tree that was struck by lightening.

▼ The solitary pine and a rough stone boulder containing Pirandello's ashes in contrada Caos.

▲ *Ephebus of Agrigento,* a kouros of 480 BC found in a cistern near the Temple of Demeter.

Province of Agrigento

■ Porto Empedocle

Porto Empedocle became a tourist attraction when Andrea Camilleri used the town as the setting for his detective stories centered on *Police Comissioner Montalbano*, calling it by the fictional name of Vigata. Camilleri was born here (his commissioner loves the local *arancini* or rice balls and the blue African sea) and today, in homage to the commissioner and his creator, the city has adopted the name of Vigata.

◄ Coat of arms of Charles V.

The illustrious Agrigentine philosopher Empedocles was born here in the fifth century BC, and in 1863, in his honor, *Marina di Girgenti* became Porto Empedocle. The harbor is no longer as important as it was and mostly serves the fishermen and as connection for the Pelagian Islands. The economy of the town depends on the cultivation of almonds and grapes.

The history of Porto Empedocle is connected to the sea. In the sixteenth century Charles V had a fortress, the **Torre di Carlo**, built on the sea to control the pirates. In 1749 the millenary stones of the temple of the Olympian Zeus were used for the construction of a new pier. The **Chiesa Madre** with its lavish decor was built between 1665 and 1790. To be seen in the outskirts is the first-century AD **Roman Villa of Durrueli** with traces of mosaics on the floors and parts of the peristyle.

▼ The Tower of Charles.

◄ The Chiesa Madre
of Palma di Montechiaro.

falling sheer to the sea.
The manor was built by
the Chiaramonte in the
fourteenth century and
two centuries later be-
came the property of the
Tomasi di Lampedusa
family. There is a marble
statue of the *Madonna
of Montechiaro* by Anto-
nello Gagini in the small
chapel inside.

■ Palma di Montechiaro

P alma di Montechiaro is the *Donnafugata* described by Giuseppe Tomasi di Lampedusa in his novel *Il Gattopardo (The Leopard)*. The
town was founded by Prince Carlo
Tomasi, an ancestor of the author,
in 1637. Many curious tourists come
to see the splendid **Palazzo Tomasi**
with its fine wooden ceilings. Also of
note are the Baroque **Chiesa Madre**
by the architect Angelo Italia, in white
stone preceded by a staircase, the
Benedictine Convent with its "*humble rude parlatory*",
still housing the nuns,
now skilful pastry-ma-
kers, and, three kilo-
meters away, the **Ca-
stle of Montechiaro**

■ Licata

A coastal city with a harbor, Licata
lies in the fertile valley at the
mouth of the Salso River at the foot
of the Montagna di Licata. The economy of this city of forty thousand inhabitants depends on agriculture,
on its port and in the last few years
on tourism.
With its lovely long beach of golden
sand, the town is taken by storm in
summer and is Baroque with an Islamic soul in the dwellings and nar-

► The coast
of Agrigento.

▲ The beach of the Mollarella at Licata.

row streets and lanes that lead to the port. Nothing except a few vestiges found in excavations remains of the ancient *Phintias* founded in 280 BC by the Agrigento tyrant Phintias. They can be seen together with prehistoric and Roman finds and paintings in the **Archaeological Museum** now housed in the former Cistercian **Convent della Badia** or **Santa Maria del Soccorso**. Licata's golden period was under Arab domination when the Saracens revolutionized agriculture with new crops, and it continued to expand with Frederick II who declared it state property in 1234 and built imposing castles of which practically nothing remains.

Piazza Progresso is the heart of the city, with the **Town Hall**, a fine Art Nouveau building designed in 1935 by Ernesto Basile. The fifteenth-century **Chiesa Madre di Santa Maria La Nuova** is on *Corso Vittorio Emanuele*, the main street of Licata. With a nave and two aisles, it has a wooden *Crucifix* in one of the chapels. Sup-

posedly the Turks tried to burn it more than once in past centuries. The thirteenth-century **Church and Convent of the Carmine** was restored in Baroque style by the architect Giovanni Biagio Amico. Ten eighteenth-century medallions with *Stories of the Old and New Testament* adorn the interior. The small **Cloister** still has its Gothic-Chiaramontano portal.

■ Naro

Of ancient foundations, Naro is a name that comes from the Greek *Naron*, meaning river. Frederick II made it a royal city and subsequently it became a possession of the Chiaramonte signoria.

Old Naro is at the top of a hill, while the modern city developed, in a disorderly way, along the slopes. Naro is prevalently agricultural and like the nearby Canicatti produces and exports the white table grapes, known as *Italia*.

Naro is Baroque, but Roman Baroque rather than the imaginative Baroque

▲ *Italia*, the white grapes produced in Canicattì.

of Ragusa. *Via Dante*, the main street with its palaces and churches, separates the upper city from the lower. The buildings include the seventeenth-century **Chiesa Madre**, subsequently restored, with bas-reliefs and sculpture on the facade and statues by the Gagini family inside, the **Church of the SS. Salvatore** with a splendid portal, and the **Church of San Nicolò** preceded by a lavish staircase. The noble palaces of Naro reveal the pomp and wealth of a past that has vanished, such as the fine **Palazzo Giacchetto** built in the fifteenth century while **Palazzo Morillo** dates to the eighteenth century, and the square keep with cylindrical towers with two-light openings are all that remain of the Gothic **Castello Chiaramonte**.

Christian burial grounds called "*grotto of the marvels*" were found in Contrada Canale south of the city.

■ Canicattì

Canicattì was built around a castle on a hill, and is a charming amphitheater-shaped medieval agricultural town, growing grapes, particularly the prized white table variety known as *Italia*. Canicattì, with over thirty-five thousand inhabitants, dedicates the *Sagra dell'uva*, one of the loveliest rural fiestas in all Sicily, to the grape.

The name of the town comes from the Arab *al-Qatah* or *Ayn-at-tin* (mud spring) and it became a feud of prince Bonanno who brought in confraternities and religious orders.

In addition to the rather run-down **Castle**, don't miss the **Church of the Spirito Santo** with a Baroque facade and the eighteenth-century **Chiesa Madre**, dedicated to Saint Pancrazio, with a facade that was reconstructed in the early twentieth century by Ernesto Basile.

■ Aragona

Aragona is a hamlet that was created around 1600 on a hill, in an arid yellow sulfurous countryside, by Count Baldasarre Naselli who named it after his mother, Beatrice Aragona Branciforte.

After a visit to the seventeenth-century **Chiesa Madre** with its fine eighteenth-century wooden *Crèche* with life-size figures, a visit to the **Nature Reserve of Macalube** is a must. Four kilometers from the center of town, the reserve covers 1256 hectares in a surreal environment of white and grey clay, a lunar landscape with springs of methane gas erupting and forming countless small cones, known as "*vulcanelli*" or baby volcanoes, ten or fifteen centimeters high spitting mud. What the inhabitants call *occhiu di Macalubi* has always aroused the curiosity of travelers and while they fasciated the philosopher Plato, Guy de Maupassant, who visited Italy in 1885, compared the *vulcanelli* to the boils of a disease.

▼ The Vulcanelli of Macalube.

▲▼ The Necropolis at Sant'Angelo Muxaro and the Tomb of the Queen on Mount Adranone.

■ Sant'Angelo Muxaro

The Sicano *Kamikos*, modern Sant'Angelo Muxaro, is at the top of a barren hill to the left of the Platani River, thirty kilometers from Agrigento. Traditionally it was founded by Daedalus for King Kokalos. Refounded in 1500 by the Aragona Pignatelli nobility, who made it their feud, Sant'Angelo Muxaro is now a quiet hamlet of a thousand souls who live on agriculture.

To see is the **necropolis** with the *tholo* (loculi) excavated in the rock along the slopes of the hill. Some date to the tenth century BC while others are of the eighth century BC.

► Ruins on the Acropolis on Monte Adranone.

The so-called **Tomb of the Prince** is monumental, a circular room topped by a dome, transformed centuries later into a Christian temple by the Byzantines.

Excavations have brought to light the vestiges of a Greek sixth-century BC city on **MONTE ADRANONE**, only seven kilometers from Sambuca di Sicilia. It was founded by Selinunte on a previous Sicano, then Punic, settlement. Thre is a **necropolis**, with the large **tomb of the Queen**, *walls* and the remains of a *city gate*, a quarter with vestiges of dwellings as well as circular prehistoric huts, a Punic *shrine* and on the **acropolis** the remains of a Punic *temple*, and what the archaeologists have called a **farm**, a rectangular building with a courtyard onto which many rooms for work and religious rites opened.

■ Sciacca

Sciacca is a pleasant town on a terrace overlooking the African sea, famous for its fine beaches of golden sand, its spas, carnival and ceramics. In Sciacca carnival is a nineteenth-century tradition that centers on a bonfire where a marionette known as *Beppe Nappa* is burned, at which time candy, wine and grilled sausages are offered to the participants.

Rising up over the town is Monte San Calogero – named after a hermit from

▼ The splendid sea of Sciacca.

Constantinople who withdrew there – with therapeutic clouds of water vapor rising from caves in the mountain. The Romans named it **Termae Selinuntinae** since the city was founded by Selinunte as a military outpost on a Phoenician settlement. Pliny, Cicero and Diodorus all came to the baths, and praised the beneficial and therapeutic properties of the water.

The mountain is a favorite site with tourists who come not only for the *"stufe vaporose"*, natural steam baths, but also to the **Shrine** dedicated to **Calogero,** a fifth-century saint who converted the pagans living in the grottoes (Agrigento, Sciacca and Naro both claim the saintly hermit as their own).

Under Arab dominion the city became a flourishing agricultural and trading center. Whether the Arabs called it *Shaqqa*, a name found in Syria, or *Shakka*, a Lebanese word that means crack, or *Syac*, meaning bath or *Xacca* which then, from the Latin became Sciacca is a moot question. In any case this delightful town has maintained its Arab features in the square houses, the labyrinthine lanes, staircases, flowering courtyards and patios, full of life.

To be seen in Sciacca are the Cathedral, the Palazzo Steripinto and *Piazza Scandaliato*. The view from the piazza of the sea and the potters' quarter at the foot of the historical center with its shops, open-air workshops and kilns, is fascinating.

The ceramics of Sciacca have a long tradition. "Diodorus Siculus appre-

► Sciacca from the sea.

ciated the quality and the shapes", and it flourished under the Arabs, who as at Caltagirone, introduced the glazing technique.

The aristocratic **Palazzo Steripinto** was built in the sixteenth century by the Lucchesi family in the then fashionable Catalan-Gothic style. The facade is faced with diamond-point ashlars and tracery and two-light openings.

The **Cathedral**, dedicated to Saint Mary Magdalene, overlooks *Piazza Don Minzoni*. Built in 1108 for the countess Giulietta, it was almost completely rebuilt in 1656. The three apses are Norman, while the facade, a Baroque reconstruction, is decorated with five marble statues by Antonino and Gian Domenico Gagini. The frescoed Latin-cross interior has a splendid *Madonna della Catena* in the fifth chapel on the right, possibly by Francesco Laurana or Giuliano Mancino.

◄ Picking oranges at Ribera.

A few kilometers from Sciacca is **RIBERA**, a locality famed for its strawberries and oranges of a *Brazilian* variety, oval in form, juicy and sweet. The town, surrounded by orange groves, is where the Italian statesman Francesco Crispi (1818-1901) was born. His house can be visited. In Ribera, named after Maria Afan de Ribera, wife of the feudal prince Guglielmo Moncada di Paternò, who founded the agricultural hamlet in 1627, worthy of note are the eighteenth-century **Chiesa Madre** and the **Castle of Poggio Diana**, built in the fourteenth century by Guglielmo Peralta.

■ Eraclea Minoa

The solitary ruins of the ancient Heraclea Minoa are on a hill at the beginning of Capo Bianco, a promontory of white rock falling sheer to the sea below, to the left of the *Halykes* River (Platani). Diodorus Siculus says it was founded by King Minos during his search for Daedalus and was therefore called *Minoa*. It is also said that the tyrant Theron discovered the tomb of the king and returned the bones to the Cretans. In the sixth century BC the city was colonized by the Spartans of Euryleon and the name Eraclea was added in homage to Herakles.

The proscenium of the relatively well-preserved fourth-third century BC **Theater** faces the sea and on summer nights the magic of this choreographic white theater lives again. In the residential zone portions of the **city walls** and **dwellings** of the archaic period have been brought to light. The finds are in the small **Antiquarium** at the entrance to the site.

► The white Theater of Eraclea Minoa.

► The famous reefs of *Scala dei Turchi* at Realmonte.

Along the coast not far from Agrigento and Porto Empedocle is **REALMONTE**, a vacation site with a spectacular amphitheater-shaped coast – *Scala dei Turchi* – with white terraced reefs, eroded by the wind and the water, rising from a green sea that changes to blue after a hundred meters. Pirates used to land here, hence the name.

▲ The sea and the beach of Guitgia in Lampedusa.

■ Pelagie (Pelagian Islands)

The Greek *Pelagos*, "high-sea" islands, or Isole Pelagie include Lampedusa, Linosa and the rock of Lampione, a distant archipelago, further south than south, in the midst of the Mediterranean and closer to Africa than Italy. Five thousand inhabitants normally live on the islands, a number which is quintuplicated in summer with hosts of vacationers looking for a vacation that renews body and soul.

Wild and uncontaminated, the blinding light is African as are the sun and the sirocco or south-east wind. The transparent sea varies in color from green to blue and is rich in marine flora and fauna and sometimes one seems to be in the tropics.

LAMPEDUSA is the name of both the island furthest south and of the town, a small harbor with the beach of **Guitgia** and bougainvillea climbing up over the houses. In the interior, as in Pantelleria, the typical square Arab houses with small domes, the *dammusi*, the envy of tourists, can still be found.

Lampedusa is also a **Nature Reserve** for migrating birds and the loggerhead turtles which come in June to lay hundreds of eggs in this lovely and most photographed bay of Lampedusa, the **Isola dei Conigli**. The islet, named after the wild rabbits, is connected to the beach by a bar of white sand. Boulders separate rabbit beach from the charming **Cala Pulcino**, which, together with **Cala Greca** and **Cala Croce**, is a favorite with tourists. Lampedusa, which belonged to the Tomasi princes, has countless hidden grottoes which delight the many scuba divers who come every year.

Pilgrimages come all year round to the **Shrine of the Madonna di Porto**

► The loggerhead turtles in the shoals of Lampedusa.

Salvo set in a pretty garden. Originally a religious building for the survivors of shipwrecks where they were given water and food, the shrine is dear to Christians and Muslims.

LINOSA, the smallest island, only eleven kilometers around, is characterized by its pastel-colored houses. It is of volcanic origin with dark rocks falling sheer to the sea and has few beaches. Plants and vineyards flourish in the craters of its three main peaks, **Monte Nero, Monte Rosso** and **Monte Vulcano.**

Those who want to go swimming and snorkeling in the marvelous underwater world of Linosa, populated by fish of all kinds and large sponges, head for **Cala Pozzolana di Ponente** or **Punta Calcarella** or the natural pools of sky-blue water, between **Punta Beppe Tuccio** and the **Faraglioni,** or **Fili** with its red and black rocks and where seagulls nest, or the **beach of the Sicchitella** at Punta Calcarella.

▼ The picturesque colored houses of Linosa.

CALTANISSETTA

After feudalism was suppressed in 1812, in 1818 Caltanissetta became the capital of the Nissena province. Before that it was the mining capital for the extraction of sulfur in the triangle with Enna and Agrigento as the two other points. Four fifths of the world production came from here until competition from America led to the closure of the mines. These have now been turned into parks of industrial archaeology and ethno-anthropological museums in memory of the back-breaking work in the shafts.

Saffron is the color of the city and its province, in the blazing sun, the wheat, sulfur. Even the sirocco, the hot south-east wind, turns yellow. In the midst of wheat-covered plains and hills, Goethe was stunned by their vastness, defining them a *desert of fertility*.

The entire province was a land of great feuds and landed estates ruled over by powerful Sicilian lords and barons, Moncada di Paternò, Chiaramonte, Ventimiglia, Lanza di Trabia, who built castles, palaces, villas and entire villages. Count Roger was the first, after the conquest in 1086, to break up the lands and he donated them above all to the religious.

The name derives from the Arab *Qal'at Nisa*, castle of the women, but its history according to Thucydides is older. In 427 BC Nissa was already a flourishing Syracusan colony and, before that, it was the dominion of Sicani and Siculi.

The heart of the city is *Piazza Garibaldi*, with the modern **Triton Fountain**, and some of the most important monuments, the Cathedral and the Church of San Sebastiano, and is where the two principal streets, *Corso Umberto* and *Corso Vittorio Emanuele*, cross.

The **Cathedral**, built between 1570 and 1622 and rebuilt in the nine-

▼ The fertile Nissena countryside.

teenth century, is dedicated to Saint Michael Archangel and Saint Mary the New (Santa Maria la Nova). The interior is a glory of eighteenth-century stuccoes and frescoes by the Flemish painter Wilhelm Borremans, considered his masterpiece, such as the lovely altarpiece with the *Virgin and Saints*, while the **Treasury** houses an elaborate fifteenth-century monstrance.

The Baroque **Church of San Sebastiano** with a three-tiered facade, opposite the Cathedral, is dedicated to

▲▼ The Cathedral of Santa Maria la Nova and the apses of the Abbey of Santo Spirito.

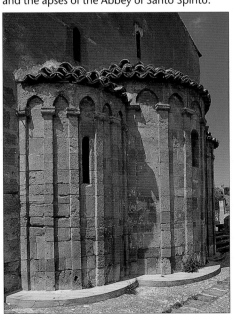

the saint who freed the city from the plague. It was begun in the sixteenth century but not completed until the nineteenth. The seventeenth-century **Church of Sant'Agata** built by the Jesuits at the top of a flight of stairs is more austere. The interior is decorated with frescoes, polychrome marble inlays and numerous works of art. Of note is the altarpiece with the *Martyrdom of Saint Agatha* by Agostino Scilla and a *Saint Ignatius in Glory* by Ignazio Marabitti.

Nothing but ruins, known to the locals as *le murra di l'ancili* (walls of the angels), remain of the old Arab fortress **Castello di Pietrarossa**, from where the Saracens dominated the valley of the Salso. The **Abbey of Santo Spirito**, the oldest and perhaps loveliest church of Caltanissetta, is three kilometers from the city. The Abbey was founded by Count Roger and his wife Adelasia and is a Romanesque rural parish church with three apses dating to 1151. The splendid *baptismal font* inside dates to the twelfth century.

Numerous finds from the neighboring necropoli are in the **Archaeological Museum**: ceramics, clay statuettes and precious funeral furnishings of various periods. Minerals, sulfur and gesso crystals, rocks and fossils are to be seen in the **Museo Mineralogico e della Zolfara**.

▼ The Trabonella sulfur mine, now Park of Industrial Archaeology.

Province of Caltanissetta

■ Sabucina

The archaeological site of Sabucina is on a hill, eight kilometers from Caltanissetta. There are Bronze Age necropoli, primitive circular huts, a small terracotta temple, a Greek sanctuary, dwellings and portions of Greek walls dating to the seventh-sixth cent. BC. There are also remains of a Roman village with a few buildings and two necropoli. Objects recovered during the excavations are to be found in the **Antiquarium**.

■ Mussomeli

Mussomeli with its eleven thousand inhabitants on the sulfur-bearing highlands has been an agricultural center since Arab times. The city was founded in the fourteenth century as Manfreda, under the feudal dynasty of Manfred III of Chiaramonte. The historical center in the old *Terravecchia* quarter is still intact, with the opulent **Palazzo del Principe** and the **Chiesa Madre** built in 1300s but not finished till three hundred years later by the famous Lanza di Trabia family who became the "signoria of the town" in 1548 and built convents and churches and other buildings.

The principal monument in Mussomeli is still its monumental **Castle** perched up high at seven hundred and eighty meters on a cliff, two kilometers from the historical center. It was built in 1370 by Manfredi Chiaramonte on an Arab fort and was restored in 1910 by the Lanza di Trabia descendents. It still has its crenellated walls, bifores, vaulting with ogee arches and Gothic portals. Particularly majestic is the **Hall of the Barons** which in 1378, on the death of Frederick III of Aragon, hosted the famous council of the four powerful Vicars of the island to divide up the rule over Sicily. There is a fine copy of the sixteenth-century sculpture of the *Madonna della Catena* in the small **Chapel** in the castle.

The locals love to tell tourists the story of how Baron Cesare Lanza lived the last years of his life secluded in the castle, full of remorse because he had killed his daughter, the beautiful Baroness of Carini who had betrayed her husband Don Vincenzo La Grua.

◄ The Castle of Mussomeli.

■ Gela

Athena Lindia was the protectress of the Geloi who lived in the fertile "geloi fields', and they erected magnificent temples to their goddess. The origins of Gela go far back in time and it has a glorious past. I was founded in 688 BC at the mouth of the Gela River by colonists from Rhodes and Crete and was repeatedly destroyed but always flourished anew. Mentioned by Virgil in the *Aeneid*, beloved by Aeschylus, the tragic poet who died there in 456 BC the city was governed by the enlightened tyrant Hippocrates who defeated the powerful Syracusans in 492 BC, at the height of Gela's economic and cultural prosperity. Today the city along the southern coast of Sicily, washed by the African

▼◄ The Acropolis of Gela
and the solitary column,
all that remains of the Doric Temple.

sea and with beaches of sand dunes, has been ruined by wildcat building projects and by the smoke stacks and drills of the petrochemical industry that have transformed the panorama of the city on its two hills, Molino a Vento and Capo Soprano. Reminders of its great past are the archaeological site and museum.

In the *Parco della Rimembranza* (Memory Park), at **Molino a Vento**, where there was once an **Acropolis** divided by a *plateia* (main street), are the columns of a sixth-century

◀ ▲ Terra-cotta statuette of the sixth cent. BC and fifth-cent. BC antefix in the Archaeological Museum.

BC temple dedicated to Athena, the base of another Doric temple dating to the fifth century BC and the remains of the sixth-century BC circle of fortified walls.

At **Capo Soprano**, facing the sea, are 300 meters of perfectly preserved wall, part of the original **Greek fortifications** built by Timoleon after 339 BC in stone and brick. Not far off are the **Hellenistic baths**, two rooms with terra-cotta tubs of the fourth century BC. The **Archaeological Museum** contains more than four thousand objects found during the excavations. Those from Gela's golden period, archaic Greek, are particularly lovely, such as the *head of a woman with kalathos* of the fifth century BC or the many clay *statuettes* or those of *De-*

meter and *Athena*, the one of a sixth-century BC *Kore* with an incense burner on her head as well as pottery and Gorgon masks.

Only eight kilometers from town is the **Nature Reserve of Biviere di Gela**, a natural coastal lake covering one hundred and twenty hectares and managed by the Lipu (Italian League for the Protection of Birds). A varicolored flora grows in the three hundred and thirty-one hectares of the reserve, but it is above all the habitat of two hundred species of aquatic birds who pass through or come to winter.

► Flora and fauna of Biviere di Gela.

ENNA

◄ Holy Week procession.

Cicero called this city at the center of the island in the heart of the hinterland the navel of Sicily. Enna stands nine hundred and forty-three meters above sea-level and is surrounded by softly rolling hills where fava beans and grain are grown. Under Rome it was the granary of the empire. Since 1926 Enna has been the capital of the province. Like its countryside, the city is a monochrome yellow. Unlike the other Sicilian cities, it is solitary and keeps to itself, bitter but with a noble dignity, the faithful custodian of traditions. It reveals one of the many faces and souls of Sicily. In Enna myth is interwoven with history and the divinities, Ceres or Demeter, Persephone or Prosperpina, have triumphed and, in a certain sense still do in the many images of the Madonna, as on the Feast of July 2 for the patron saint *Maria Santissima della Visitazione*, a choral event in which the ancestral rite of the transportation of Ceres' wagon is celebrated and everyone dresses in white.

Before becoming an autonomous Greek city in the sixth century BC, Enna was inhabited by the Sicani and then the Siculi. For the Romans who freed it from the Carthaginian yoke in 259 BC it was *Castrum Hennae*. The Byzantines were followed by the

▼ The countryside around Enna.

Arabs in 859 who made *Qasr Yànnah* a rich agricultural center. The Normans and the Swabians then built churches and turned it into a stronghold of their kingdom.

The **Castello di Lombardia** built by Frederick II in 1160 on a pentagonal ground plan is an imposing structure on a rocky spur. One of the most important in Sicily, it is surrounded by walls and square towers while inside it is one courtyard after another with a church and the emperor's apartments. One of the loveliest panoramas in Sicily ranging over the valleys up to Mount Etna can be had

◄▼ The imposing Castello di Lombardia.

from the crenellated keep of the castle, the **Pisan Tower**. On the **Rocca di Cerere** near the castle are the ruins of the temple dedicated to the *great Mediterranean Mother*, Ceres or Demeter, of whose worship Enna was the center. **Frederick's Tower**, built as a lookout over the valley, is octagonal and twenty-four meters high, with great halls inside.

The city's **Cathedral**, a mixture of styles, is dedicated to Mary and was built in 1307 by Eleanor of Aragon

▲ Frederick's Tower.

and then rebuilt after the fire of 1446. The transept and the three apses are original. A sixteenth-century portal with over it a marble bas-relief of *Saint Martin and the poor man* leads into the three-aisled Basilica, richly decorated with statues and paintings. Particularly fine, in a niche, is the painting of the *Visitation* by Filippo Paladino. The golden litter, in the right apse, holds the fifteenth-century sculpture of the *Madonna of the Visitation*.

The **Alessi Museum** contains the seventeenth-century *golden crown of the Madonna of the Visitation* studded with rubies and diamonds, as well as the **Cathedral Treasury**. The

◄▲ Archaeological finds in
the Museum of Enna in Palazzo Varisano.

Archaeological Museum in **Palazzo Varisano** contains finds from the territory of Enna: grave goods dating to the third-second millennium BC from the neighboring necropoli, antefixes, kraters, pottery and clay statuettes.

LAGO DI PERGUSA nine kilometers from Enna is a natural lake of brackish water mentioned by Ovid in his *Metamorphoses*. It was here that the lovely Proserpine (Persephone or Kore) picking crocus flowers was carried away by Pluto who took her to Hades. A cave hidden in the eucalyptus trees – so says the myth – is the grotto to which the god of the underworld took the maiden while her mother Demeter threatened to let agriculture die. A recently built auto and motorcycle racing track around its shores has, with its racket, stripped some of the poetry and magic from this lake which on certain days, for a few hours, turns a violet hue.

▼ The lake of Pergusa.

Province of Enna

■ Piazza Armerina

Located on three hills in a fertile countryside, this is one of the best-known and most visited towns in Sicily thanks to the mosaics of *Villa del Casale*, considered the eighth marvel, and also to the *Palio dei Normanni*, a tournament that takes place every year on August 13-14 in costumes that evoke the entry into the city of the troops of Roger Guiscard de Hauteville in 1087. In the mid-thirteen hundreds when the banner he had given the town was carried to the church, the plague which had been raging died out and the banner, bearing the image of the Madonna, was credited with this miracle.

Piazza Armerina is full of palaces, now in disrepair, churches and convents in a historical center that is an endless up and down of winding lanes that hide flowering courtyards. The **Church** and **Convent of San Rocco** or **of Fundrò** with a carved sandstone portal overlook *Piazza Garibaldi*, where all the roads meet, while the fine Baroque **Cathedral** dominates from the top of the steep Via Cavour. Built in 1627, it is the most expressive religious monument of Piazza Armerina despite the many alterations. The majolica dome was added in the eighteenth century while the

▲▼ Panorama of Piazza Armerina and the tournament of the Palio dei Normanni.

fifteenth-century bell tower has two pairs of Gothic-Catalan windows. Dedicated to Our Lady of the Assumption, the Cathedral houses many works in its white and blue interior including the fine Byzantine icon of the Madonna delle Vittorie given by Pope Nicholas II to Count Roger, a *Crucifix* painted on both sides by Pietro Ruzzolone and an *Assumption of the Virgin*, a canvas by Filippo Paladino.

The **Palazzo Trigona Canicarao**, once residence of the great land-owning baron who sponsored the building of the cathedral, also overlooks *Piazza del Duomo*. The Romanesque jewel of the **Priorato di Sant'Andrea**, a small medieval church with three apses and good frescoes, lies along the way to Villa del Casale, passing through *Piazza Vecchia*.

■ Villa del Casale

Five kilometers from the historical center of Piazza Armerina is the Roman Villa of Casale, an archaeological gem, the magnificent testimony of Roman civilization in Sicily, and justly considered the eighth marvel. Since 1997 it has been a UNESCO World Heritage Site.

Dating to the third-fourth century AD, the Roman villa is a triumph of luxury, with a refined taste for opulence. There is an exotic flavor to the mosaics that cover the floors of the forty rooms in the three buildings set on terraces due to the layout of the land. The buildings are connected to each other by courtyards and corri-

▼ ► The *Triclinium* and columns of the Atrium of the Villa del Casale.

dors and cover an area of three thousand five hundred square meters in the midst of a flourishing green countryside. It is probably on the site of the antique station of *Philosophiana*. The villa and the surrounding large estates may have belonged to Procopius Populonia, who imported wild animals from Africa for the circus games in Rome, or to the aristocratic Maximianus Herculius, forced to resign from the imperial tetrarchy by Diocletian. Whoever he was, he was refined and loved beauty.

The first rooms to be met with after the **Atrium** with its fountain are the **Thermal Baths** with the *frigidarium*, an octagonal room, and the *tepida-*

▲ Mosaic depicting "Autumn" in the Room of the Four Seasons.

▲ *Diaeta* of the Small Hunt.

▲ Mosaic in the Vestibule of the Small Circus.

rium, with mosaics of marine scenes. There are no mosaics in the three *calidaria*. The **Peristyle** is a rectangular courtyard where guests were received and taken to the **Vestibule** with its fine mosaic of a servant greeting the guests with an olive branch. Mosaic decorations depicting the circus races run along the long room, with an apse at either end. Along the south side of the peristyle are a series of smaller rooms, including the **Room of the Small Hunt** with highly detailed hunting and banquet scenes. The mosaics in the **Corridor of the Great Hunt**, sixty-four meters long, betray African influences and depict safaris with men capturing wild beasts and then shipping them via sea to Rome. A mosaic in the same room may be a portrait of the owner of the villa, shown between two soldiers and wearing an elegant cloak. The **Cubicle of Love** with an erotic scene was part of the private apartments

▼ Detail of "Africa" in a lunette in the Corridor of the Great Hunt.

◄ *Erotic scene* in the Cubicle of Love.

■ Morgantina

The entrancing archaeological site of ancient mysterious Morgantina is four kilometers from **AIDONE**, an agricultural town in a green valley between two heights. Morgantina was founded by the Morgeti an Italic tribe, in 850 BC, destroyed four hundred years later by Ducetius a national leader who welded the native communities of eastern Sicily into a federation.

When it was conquered by Agathocles, tyrant of Syracuse, it became a prosperous Greek city. Morgantina later allied itself with the Carthaginians and in the second century BC was the object of Roman revenge who handed it over to the Iberian mercenary Moericus.

The **Agorà**, as in all Greek cities, was the center of public life. The one in Morgantina is on two levels, separa

as was the **Room of Arion** with a mosaic depicting the *musician sitting on the back of a dolphin*, a basilica for receptions and audiences, and the dining room, the **Triclinium**, with mosaics dedicated to the *labors of Hercules*. At the end of the long corridor is the **Room of the Palestrite** or **of the Ten Girls**, the most famous in the villa, with mosaics depicting ten pretty girls in daring costumes that precede the bikini by sixteen centuries.

▼ The famous mosaic of *The Ten Girls in Bikinis*.

ted by a trapezoidal staircase with fourteen steps, the **Ekklesiasterion** where the citizens gathered in assembly. Markets, shops and granaries, the **macellum** and a **gymnasium** are on the upper level, while on the lower level, perfectly preserved, is the splendid fourth-century BC **theater** with room for over a thousand spectators.

Not far from the theater was the **Sanctuary of Demeter and Persephone** with remains of basins, altars and a well, and the patrician dwellings to which the floor mosaics bear witness. One of the finest is the **House of Ganymede** with a brightly colored mosaic of the third century BC depicting the *rape of Ganymede*, cup bearer of the gods, carried off by Zeus in the form of an eagle. The fine statue of a sensual *Venus* with clinging garments, two meters high (5th cent. BC), bought by the Getty Museum of Malibù in 1988, as well as the ancient coins in the same museum all come from Morgantina. The **Archaeological Museum** of **Aidone** – first stopover in getting to know Morgantina – hopes to get them back one day. The permanent exhibition is in the former **Capuchin Convent** with numerous

▼ The Agorà of Morgantina.

◄ Mosaic floor in Morgantina.

Rebuilt by Frederick II, Centuripe rose up against the emperor, who destroyed it in 1232. Rebuilt anew, it was then destroyed by Charles of Anjou in 1268, and finally refounded in the sixteenth century by Francesco Moncada.

The Baroque **Chiesa Madre** in Centuripe is painted pink and white and the interesting **Archaeological Museum** contains over three thousand pieces, the artistic fund of the city from the seventh century BC up to the Middle Ages. The finds including clay statues of women, antefixes in the shape of the head of a maenad, a lion mask and a Gorgon head, as well as statues and busts, such as the charming one of *Persephone with a diadem*, and of course vases, kraters, plates and even artifacts and the remains of huts dating to the Bronze age.

■ Centuripe

The road to Centuripe runs along through dense citrus groves. The town lies at an altitude of seven hundred and fifty meters, facing Etna and, in virtue of its fine location, well merited Cicero's calling it the *balcony city*. Its history of destruction and rebirth goes back to the native Siculi who called it *Kentoripa*. In the fifth century BC it became Greek and with the Romans was one of the most fertile and richest cities in the area. Its decline and then the end began with the war of the Roman condottieri Ottavianus and Sextus Pompeius.

vestiges of the *Temple of the Augustal* in eastern Centuripe date to the Augustan age, as do the ruins of a *Nymphaeum* and the fine marble *heads of Hadrian and Medusa*, as well as clay statuettes of the third century BC.

■ Agira

Agira is a hard-working agricultural town of barely nine thousand inhabitants, on the top of a hill in the sulfur-bearing upland, but with an age-old history. Myth says that Hercules stayed here many times and in his honor the city organized festivals and games. The historian Diodorus Siculus was born here in 90 BC and in his forty volume *Universal History* he praised the beauty of its theater (no longer extant), comparing it to that of Syracuse. Philip of Agira known as the Syrian monk evangelized Agira and made it an important religious center in the region.

It flourished under the Siculi, who called it *Agyrion*, and it became ever more prosperous in 339 BC with the Greek colonists. Despite Cicero's praises, calling the citizens *summi oratores e viri forte*, Agira's decline began with the Roman domination and it was not until the Arabs and Normans came that it prospered anew, and Charles V bestowed the title of *città demaniale* upon Agira, providing it with special privileges.

Agira still betrays its Arab origins in the layout of the historical center overshadowed by the towers of the **Swabian castle** built on an Arab fort. Not to be missed are some of the churches, such as the sixteenth-century **Church of Sant'Antonio da Padova** which contains a magnificent painting of Flemish school of the *Deposition of Christ*, and the twelfth-century **Church** and **Convent of San Filippo** or **Chiesa Madre**. Rebuilt, the church contains a fifteenth-century triptych and a chased silver urn with the relics of the saint in addition to a wooden *Crucifix* by Fra' Umile da Petralia.

▼ View of Agira.

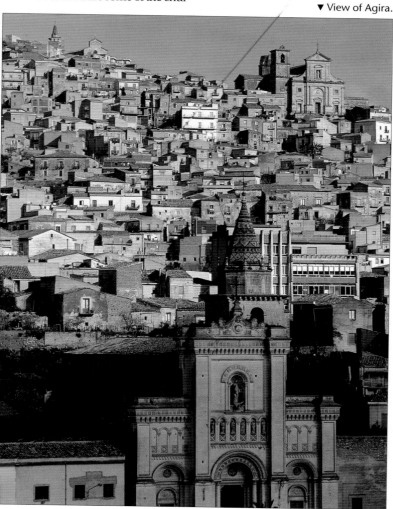

RAGUSA

▲ Carob beans grow in the province of Ragusa.

he Baroque triumphs in Ragusa, a peaceful provincial city with seventy thousand inhabitants. Ragusa *supra* was rebuilt from scratch on the plateau after the earthquake of 1693, while Ragusa *iusù* is the ancient Ibla rebuilt on the old medieval layout. The two cities are united by a staircase of three hundred and thirty steps, *Santa Maria delle Scale*, three bridges and a zigzag road, *Corso Mazzini*, built under Fascism to join the two. There is something prodigious about the Baroque setting here, in an ocher-colored limestone, gilded by the African sun. It is the architecture which identifies and unites the two Ragusas, created by the Church and the land-owning aristocracy in their determination to have the city rise, like the Arabian phoenix, from the rubble of the terrible earthquake of 1693 which razed it to the ground.

The Greek *Hybla Heraia*, first inhabited by the Siculi, the Greeks, Romans and Byzantines, flourished under the Arabs who revolutionized agriculture, redistributing the fallow lands and introducing new crops. Then came the Normans and around the fourteenth century the city passed to the countship of Modica. The Cabrera counts were the first to introduce the practice of emphyteusis, with the

▼ A typical corner of Ragusa Ibla.

peasants becoming small landowners and paying the feudal noble rent. This practice modified the agricultural landscape where the countryside is dotted with white farm houses and dry masonry walls set among the almond and carob trees, prickly pears and olive groves.

The old **Ragusa Ibla** is spell-binding with a tangle of buildings and narrow streets, lanes, courtyards, corners opening out in small squares that offer charming views of Baroque caprices in monuments, palaces and churches such as the lovely **Cathedral**, dedicated to Saint George, preceded by a monumental staircase that accentuates its verticality. It was built in the eighteenth century by

▼ View of Ragusa Ibla.

the Sicilian architect Rosario Gagliardi, the man behind the brilliant and opulent Baroque of Ragusa. The facade, with a convex bay at the center, has three tiers of columns and a dome on top. The interior with a nave and two side aisles contains paintings and thirteen historiated stained-glass windows with the *Martyrdom of Saint George*.

The facade of the **Church of San Giu-** seppe, similar to the cathedral, is also by Gagliardi. It has Corinthian columns and statues in its three tiers, while the oval interior is all stuccoes and frescoes. The *Glory of Saint Benedict* is in the dome.

There are two churches in the **Ibleo Gardens**, below the fortress, with an extraordinary view over the valleys reaching, if the day is clear, to the sea on the horizon. **San Giacomo** dates to the fourteenth century and has a fine wooden ceiling and a sculpture of *Saint James on horseback fighting the infidel Arabs*. The **Capuchin church** contains a triptych by Pietro Novelli, *Madonna with Saints Agatha and Agnes*. The church at the top of

▼ The typical caciocavallo cheese.

▲ Ricotta cheeses.

▲ The sumptuous Baroque of the Cathedral of San Giorgio in Ragusa Ibla.

the staircase that joins the two Ragusas is **Santa Maria delle Scale**. It was rebuilt after the earthquake of 1693 on a Cistercian church and convent of Norman times and the portal and the pulpit at the base of the bell tower belong to the original structure. Inside is a sixteenth-century terra-cotta of the school of Gagini. *Corso Italia* is the main street of **Ragusa supra,** with Gattopard-like palaces one after the other, bearing witness to memorable splendors, such as the **Palazzo Bertini** with three sym-

bolic masks at the windows (*Indifference of the pauper, Arrogance of the merchant, Pride of the nobleman*) and **Palazzo Zacco**, a profusion of carvings, almost tracery, on the lime stone. **Palazzo Cosentini** has sculptured brackets supporting the balconies and is adorned with statues. Then there is the luxurious **Palazzo Nicastro**. Both are near the **Church of Santa Maria dell'Itria** with a dome covered with majolica tiles from the neighboring Caltagirone.

San Giovanni Battista, on a hanging

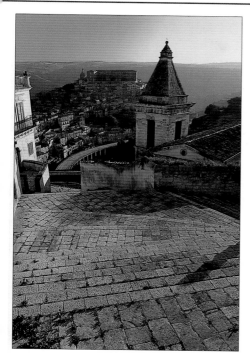

◄ View of Ragusa Ibla from Santa Maria delle Scale.

who turned a villa into a castle at the end of the nineteenth century.

The entire complex covers two thousand five hundred square meters, with a hundred and twenty-two richly furnished rooms and twelve hectares of park divided into three gardens with a thousand five hundred species of plants as well as statues and fountains. The castle has Arab origins, and was originally a small fort called *ayn as jafait* (fount of health) which was corrupted into "donnafugata" or woman fleeing because – according to a popular legend – the lovely Bianca di Navarra fled from the castle to escape from the count of Cabrera and Donna Clementina Paternò did the same, except that she ran away to join her lover Gaetano Combes de Lestrade, a relationship opposed by her uncle Corrado Arezzo.

terrace over a portico, is the **Cathedral** of Ragusa nuova, with an elegant two-tiered facade and sculptural decoration, while the interior is overflowing with stuccoes.

Finds from the Greek city of Camarina are in the **Ibleo Archaeological Museum**, in the Palazzo Mediterraneo (entrance from Via Natalelli), as well as terra-cotta statuettes, vases, Roman pottery and mosaics.

CASTELLO DI DONNAFUGATA is located seventeen kilometers from Ragusa, completely isolated and immersed in the countryside between Ragusa and the sea. This is not the one described by Tomasi di Lampedusa in his famous novel *The Leopard*, but is a patrician residence of a man of letters and collector of art, Baron Corrado Arezzo de Spuches,

► The Cathedral of San Giovanni Battista in Ragusa alta.

Province of Ragusa

■ Modica

A Baroque city, with a hundred churches and a hundred bell towers, the city of chocolate made at a very low temperature the way the Aztecs did, the city of the Modica breed of cattle, a reddish breed brought by the Arabs with a yield of milk that is limited but rich and excellent for the *dop caciocavallo cheese*; the city where Salvatore Quasimodo, poet and translator of Greek classics, was born. He was awarded the Nobel prize in 1959 and his house in *Via Posterla* is now a museum with majolica tiles with his verses hanging on the walls.

Like Ragusa, the city is divided into two parts: Modica alta or upper Modi-

▼◄ The Baroque Cathedral of San Giorgio and detail of the facade, masterpiece by Rosario Gagliardi.

▲ Panorama of the city with the Church of San Pietro in the foreground.

ca on the hill and, at its feet, Modica bassa, rebuilt after the earthquake of January 11, 1693.

The Modica described by Gesualdo Bufalino in his book *"Blind Argus"* as *"a pomegranate split in half"* was the *Motyka* of the Siculi, later rechristened *Mohac* by the Arabs. After the Norman domination the city became an important and powerful countship, first of the Chiaramonte and then of the Cabrera, who introduced emphyteusis, which made it one of the richest in Sicily. Discovering Modica is a delight, even if your legs may ache after climbing up and down the steep streets and steps, but the beauty of the picturesque town and its monuments make it worth while, especially after having sipped a cup of vanilla or cinnamon chocolate in one of the nineteen chocolate shops scattered throughout the city.

The Baroque **Cathedral** or **Chiesa Madre di San Giorgio** was built in the eighteenth century by Rosario Gagliardi, master of the unusual perspective and scenic solutions that characterize the Sicilian Baroque, differentiating it from Bernini's Roman Baroque. The cathedral is considered Gagliardi's masterpiece.

The Cathedral, preceded by a majestic staircase, moves scenically upwards like a tower, with a facade in three tiers and a play of concave and convex forms. The nave has two aisles on each side, and chapels and a wealth of ornamental elements, paintings and sculpture, including a canvas of *Our Lady of the Assumption* by Filippo Paladino and a sixteenth-century polyptych by Bernardino Niger illustrating the *Life of Saint George*. A fourteenth-century silver urn contains the relics of the saint. There is a meridian on the floor of the left transept and a statue of the *Madonna of the Snows* by Bartolomeo Berrettaro is in the chapel to the left of the main chapel.

The late Baroque **Church of San Pietro** is also preceded by an imposing staircase flanked by statues of the twelve

▲ The Parco della Forza necropolis at Cava d'Ispica.

Apostles. In the interior, a nave and two aisles, is a marble group of *Saint Peter and the cripple*, by Benedetto Civiletti. Behind is **San Niccolò Inferiore**, a delightful Byzantine rural parish church with frescoes. It is worth while taking a good look at the neighboring **Palazzo De Leva** and **Palazzo Manenti** for their magnificence and the imaginative decorative "capricci" with human figures and animals supporting the pot-bellied balustrades.

■ Cava d'Ispica

Not far from Modica and near the town of Ispica is a spell-binding natural spectacle where water has eaten out **necropoli** and **prehistoric caves** in the Hyblaean plateau. Known as "*Cave*" or quarries, they cover an area of twelve kilometers. The Christian cemetery is located here in this fascinating archaeological site in the midst of carob and almond trees, prickly pears and capers: the fourth-century AD **Catacomb of the Larderia**, the **Hypogeum of San Michele**, a Byzantine church, with traces of frescoes on the wall, and a *Madonna*, and the honeycomb of **troglodyte dwellings**, and other **caves** used by hermits.

■ Pozzallo

This old port station for exporting grain was a feud of the Cabrera counts. In the fourteenth century they built the imposing **Cabrera tower** to keep an eye on the pirates and it still overlooks the town.

▶ Giorgio La Pira and Pope Paul VI.

▲▶ View of Scicli,
one of the loveliest Baroque cities.

Pozzallo is a delightful hamlet at the center of a bay that stretches from the sandy *shore della Marza* up to *Punta Raganzino*. It is now a popular seaside resort, with a fine esplanade and a point of embarkation for Malta. The jurist and statesman Giorgio La Pira (1904-1977), long mayor of Florence and now in the process of being made a saint, was born here.

■ Scicli

This picturesque dreamlike town of twenty-five thousand inhabitants is located on a plain set into the rocky limestone hills of San Matteo, della Croce and del Rosario. Seen from the ruins of the Norman **castle**, Scicli looks like something from an Italian Nativity scene.

Not well known to the general tourists, it is dear to art historians who call it a pearl of the Baroque. Pier Paolo Pasolini, the film director and poet, found it enchanting and in his *Le città*

del mondo Elio Vittorini, the writer from Syracuse, called it the loveliest of Baroque cities.

Scicli leads a secluded life, and its inhabitants, craftsmen, agriculture and livestock farmers also keep to themselves. The women create magnificent bobbin lace for the hope chests of their brides. An independent and untamed spirit has always characterized these people and in 1091 they

◄ The imposing facade of Santa Maria la Nova in Scicli.

them. Men and means were few but they trusted in the protection of the Madonna. This event is reenacted every year on the last Sunday in May for the *Festa dela Madonna dei Milici,* with religious solemnities and a rejoicing crowd.

The monumental fifteenth-century **Church of Santa Maria la Nova**, later restored, is in the oldest district of Scicli, on the slopes of the San Rosario plateau. The church has a nave and four side aisles

were the only ones among the Iblei to fend off the Saracens and Turks who were attempting to reoccupy the territory in the *Piana dei Milici* from which the Normans had driven

with chapels and a dome with a deluge of stucco decorations and numerous works including a seventeenth-century *Madonna* by Filippo Paladino, a wooden statue of the *Res*

▼ View of Scicli, with the Church of San Bartolomeo in the foreground.

▲ The ruins of ancient Camarina.

urrected Christ by Benedetto Civiletti and the venerated statue of the *Madonna della Pietà* in cypress wood, thought to be Byzantine.

The setting of the **Church of San Bartolomeo**, right up against the walls of the gorge and with one of the loveliest facades in the city, is particularly scenic. **Palazzo Beneventano**, the most significant civil building in Scicli, is spectacular with its wealth of ornaments and figured brackets supporting pot-bellied balconies.

■ Marina di Ragusa

Marina di Ragusa, known up to 1928 as Mazzarelli after its eighteenth-century tower, now a ruin, is twenty-four kilometers from Ragusa. It has become a popular and fashionable seaside resort thanks to the fact that the popular television series *Il commissario Montalbano*, based on the novels by the Sicilian writer Andrea Camilleri, was filmed here. Marina di Ragusa has a long beach of fine golden sand, an azure crystalline sea, a warm sun for most of the year, and numerous restaurants and discotheques.

■ Camarina

The **archaeological site** of ancient Camarina, a city founded by Syracuse in 598 BC and then destroyed in 533 BC because it was an ally of Gela, is located at the mouth of the Ippari River. It was rebuilt by Timoleon in 339 BC and then destroyed by the Romans in 258 BC. Today it still has parts of its sixth-century BC city **walls**, seven meters high and preserved under the sand. There are also parts of a quarter called *Quadrivio* with fourth-century BC dwellings and the foundations of the fifth-century BC **Temple of Athena**, with the remains of the *tèmenos*, the sacred enclosure. Finds from the excavations that were begun in 1958 and are still in course are on exhibit in the **Antiquarium** on site. They include vases, amphorae, kraters and sarcophagi. The artifacts found at the bottom of the sea of Camarina are also there, such as the fine sixth-century bronze helmet.

SIRACUSA (Syracuse)

Pindaro and Cicero sang its praises, Plato called it the "ideal city". It was home to Aeschylus and Euripides, while Theocritus, Epicharmus, Archimedes, the Arab poet Ibn Hamdis, and the author Elio Vittorini were all born here. Siracusa, or Syracuse, is one of the loveliest cities in Sicily, tranquil and secluded, more Greek and Levantine than Greece itself, cradle of the civilization of Hellas. It is a city without time where myth and history merge. Past and present live together in a unique setting: Classic Greece, the papyrus plants of the spring, Jewish, Christian and Muslim quarters, Middle Ages, Baroque and Rococo, pleasures, tastes and customs, under a sun as relentless as the sirocco and the light.

It is a city of water and is on the wa-

◀ Dionysius the Great.

ter, with the sea, the spring of Arethusa, rivers, Ciane and Anapo, and even its names, *Syrako* and *Syrakeo* and then *Syrakousai*, refer to swamps and gushing water.

Syracuse has a powerful bond with the sea which can be seen from everywhere. The two natural inlets, Porto Grande and Porto Piccolo, are separated by the islet of Ortygia, the pulsing center of Syracuse, encircled by *Neapolis*, the archaeological district of white stones.

Thanks to economic aid from the European Union and the intellectuals, both Italian and foreign who have bought homes here, nostalgic Syracuse has awakened from its long slumber of emargination, the petro-

▼ The ocean front of Ortygia.

► Archimedes, the scientist of Syracuse.

chemical industry, and the building abuses that have violated the old quarters of *Tyche, Epipoli, Acradina*. Syracuse is once more alive with restoration and reconstruction, work yards and cultural events, tourism on the upswing and theater. It all began with the festivals and plays by classic authors promoted by the **Istituto del Dramma Antico**. Evenings when the curtain rises it is magic and the heart of the *polis* once more beats as it did three thousand years ago.

The strategic position of Syracuse was the drawing card that led to its colonization in the eighth century BC by the Corinthian Archia although it had been inhabited by indigenous peoples since the fourteenth century BC.

Syracuse soon became a powerful and rich center of culture. It rivaled Athens, by whom it was be sieged between 416-41 BC before defeating th Athenians. The tyrar Dionysius the Elder for tified the city in 405 BC building the Castello Eu rialo and turning Ortygi into a fortress. It was con quered by the Romans in 21 BC thanks to the new war ma chines invented by Archimedes, wh was killed by the soldiers even thoug the consul Marcellius had ordere that his life be spared. Charmed b the beauty of Syracuse, Marcellu gave orders to respect the sacre monuments, but this was the be ginning of its decline. Saint Paul con verted the city to Christianity in 53 after which it was taken by the Byzar tines, the Arabs in 818 and then th Normans and the Swabians, unde whom it flourished economicall and culturally until the high taxe imposed by Spain, the expulsion o the Jews, the plague and an earth quake in 1542 marked its definite de cline. After the earthquake of 169

▼ The mythical Fonte Aretusa where papyrus plants grow.

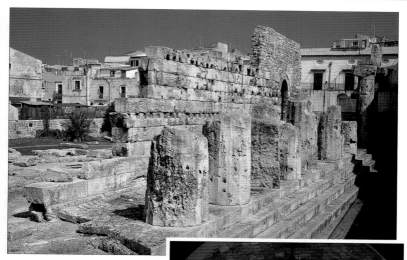

▲► The Doric Temple of Apollo and a view of medieval Ortygia.

the Baroque flourished in Syracuse as it did elsewhere, and left its mark in Ortygia. For the Syracusans **Ortygia** is *lo scoggiu*, the reef or rock that is never abandoned, a place for meeting and *passio* (promenades) on the shorefront of the **Foro Italico**, up to the fascinating terrace on the sea of **Fonte Aretusa**, a pool of fresh water with a spring, tufts of papyrus, ducks and fish, where the spirit is that of Greece. Virgil, Cicero and Ovid sang of Arethusa, a nymph of Artemis, whom the goddess transformed into a spring to save her from the river god Alpheus who had fallen in love with her. He went underground and joined her in Ortygia in the form of a river and the two waters mingled. Myth says that it was the spring that attracted the attention of the Corinthian colonizers after the predictions of the oracle of Delphi. Ortygia is best seen by walking up and down its steep narrow streets and lanes, a mixture of Greek and Islamic town planning. **Piazza Archimede** (with the **Fountain of Artemis** at the center) with cafes, restaurants, pastry shops, old shops, is the point of departure. The walk takes one past the imaginative Baroque *capricci* that decorate the palaces and churches, Arab and Aragonese buildings, the old synagogue transformed into a church and then the green sea, that enters every corner of this strip of an island barely a square kilometer in size.

The ruins of the seventh-century BC **Temple of Apollo** mark one of the entrances (the other is Porta Marina) to the elegant drawing room of Ortygia, *Piazza del Duomo*, the ancient acropolis with its sacred area, a long

▲ Piazza del Duomo with the Palazzo Senatorio, the Cathedral, the Bishop's Palace and Santa Lucia alla Badia.

irregular shape, with superb palaces, symbols of civil and religious power. **Palazzo Beneventano del Bosco** (1775) has a long wrought-iron balcony, **Palazzo Senatorio**, now Town Hall, was rebuilt by the architect Vermexio. After the **Palazzo Arcivescovile** and the **Church of Santa Lucia alla Badia** comes the **Cathedral,** a tangible example of the superposition

◄ ▼ The Cathedral and the panel with *Saint Zosimus* by Antonello da Messina in the church.

▲ *The Annunciation*
by Antonello da Messina
(Regional Gallery in Palazzo Bellomo).

of architectural styles in Syracuse. In 640 AD the Byzantines transformed it into a basilica, incorporating the fifth-century BC Temple of Athena which the Greeks had built on an earlier Siculi temple. It was then modified by the Arabs into a mosque and the Normans changed it back into a church. The fine two-tiered facade scanned by columns and statues is an eighteenth-century reconstruction by the architect Andrea Palma. The interior with its Doric columns contains sculpture and outstanding works of art such as the splendid gold-ground panel of *Saint Zosimus*, a youthful work by Antonello da Messina that has the place of honor in the *Cappella del Sacramento*. Of particular note is the fine *ciborium* (1752) on the high altar by Luigi Vanvitelli, a baptismal font of the twelfth century and a sumptuous Baroque altar by Giovanni Vermexio while a

Madonna of the Snows by Antonello Gagini is in the left apse. The *Chapel of Saint Lucy*, the dearly beloved patron saint of the Syracusans who is feted on December 13th, contains a magnificent altarpiece in addition to the silver *statue of the saint* by Pietro Rizzo.

The **Regional Gallery** is in **Palazzo Bellomo** and in addition to Nativity scenes contains vases and ceramics, sculpture, by Francesco Laurana and Antonello Gagini, and a rich **Pinacoteca** with fine works including Caravaggio's *Burial of Saint Lucy*, painted in 1608 during the artist's sojourn in Syracuse, and the diptych of the *Annunciation*, masterpiece by Antonello da Messina.

◄ The *Burial of Saint Lucy*
by Caravaggio
(Regional Gallery in Palazzo Bellomo).

The imposing **Castello Maniace** is on the point of Ortygia. Built by Frederick II in the thirteenth century as his residence on the site of the temple of Juno, it is a magnificent example of military architecture with a square ground plan and corner towers. From *Via della Maestranza*, one of the most important streets in the Middle Ages, and full of antique dealers and book shops where the intellectuals meet, a series of lanes and alleys branch out into the old Jewish district, the *Giudecca*, where a Jewish **miqwè** was recently found in the cellars of a fifteenth-century palace. It is the oldest in Europe, dating to Byzantine times, with four tubs for the ritual purification baths which the Jews (in Syracuse as early as the first century) covered with twenty meters of earth so it would not be profaned when Ferdinand's edict of 1492 drove them out.

In the same quarter signs of the rebirth of Syracuse are to be found in the newly reopened **Puppet Theater** with room for only thirty-five spectators, which stages topical events as well as the feats of the Paladini and the new **Cinema Museum**.

The **Archaeological Park of Neapolis**, the ancient quarter of Syracuse, is on the hill that the Greeks called *Temenite* and covers an area of two hundred and forty thousand square meters.

The **Theater** is one of the finest of Greek architecture, in harmony with the landscape and embracing the

▼ The Castello Maniace in Ortygia.

▲ ▶ The vaulting of the great hall of the Castello Maniace and the entrance portal.

sea and the countryside. It was built for the tyrant Hieron I by the architect Demacopos, nicknamed Myrilla for on the evening of the inauguration of the theater in 470 BC with *The Persians*, the tragedy by Aeschylus, he sprinkled the theater with *myroi*, perfumed unguents. The **Cavea** faces the sea, and is entirely dug out of the rock. A corridor, the *diazoma*, separates the upper from the lower level. With a diameter of 138 meters, 67 tiers divide it into 9 sectors and it could seat up to twenty thousand spectators. An altar, dedicated to Dionysius, the god of wine, was in the **orchestra** around which was the **choir**, while two bronze jars on the **scena** served as amplifiers.

A **terrace** dug out of the rock rises up above the theater. At its center is the **grotto of the Nymphaeum**, a sacred place for religious ceremonies, with a waterfall that came from the aqueduct. A series of votive **aedicules** where offerings were deposited was dug into the walls of the terrace, in the **Via dei Sepolcri** (where the marks of wagon wheels can still be seen). There are also Byzantine **grottoes** and **hypogea**. The Romans enlarged the scena by thirty meters for their gladiatorial games, while the Spanish used the stones and set up their water mills in the theater. Now on summer evenings the ancient Greek tradition lives once more in this lovely theater and attracts an audience from near and far.

▲ The imposing Greek Theater.

◄▲ The Grotto of the Nymphaeum
and the terrace overlooking the Theater

Used back in the fifth century BC a
quarry for white stone, the **Latomie**
a Greek word that means cutting
stone (from *litos* and *temno*), were
turned into prisons for those seven
thousand Athenians defeated in 413
BC by the Syracusans. They suffered
hunger and tribulations and were
forced to quarry rock at a depth of
forty meters until they died. Cicero

▼ The Latomia del Paradiso.

defined it as a "prison from which no escape was possible" and Plutarch tells us of a few who were freed only because they could recite from memory the verses of Euripides. Today the latomie of Syracuse are overgrown with luxuriant vegetation and dense citrus groves. What Caravaggio called the **Ear of Dionysius** is in the **Latomia del Paradiso**. This ear-shaped cavity is twenty-three meters high and sixty-five long. Chronicles report that the suspicious tyrant Dionysius used to eavesdrop on the prisoners, favored by the excellent acoustics. The **Grotta dei Cordari** next to it is another latomia occupied up to a few years ago by rope makers.

Hieron's altar was an imposing altar built as thanks to Zeus by Hieron II. The bulls sacrificed here were then roasted and served to those present. Nothing but the base is left but the measurements give us an idea of its size: 198 meters by 23 and 15 meters

▼ The Ear of Dionysius.

▲▼ The Roman amphitheater and the ruins of the imposing Castello Eurialo.

high. The Romans then built a large pool next to it, for their simulations of naval battles *(naumachie)*. The elliptical **Roman Amphitheater** of the third-fourth century AD, dug into the rock, was where the gladiatorial contests and circus games were held and was almost as large as the Colosseum and the Arena of Verona.

Epipoli was the hill district in the shape of a nail (in Greek *euryalos* and the castle built by Dionysius I to defend the city constantly besieged by the Carthaginians is known as the **Castello Eurialo**.

Now known as *Belvedere* because of the extraordinary panorama of the city and the sea to be had from the ruins of the castle, it is located only eight kilometers from the center of

► The Shrine of the Madonna delle Lacrime.

Syracuse. The fortress was built in only 5 years by 50,000 men, many of whom were slaves, and 6000 oxen were employed. The walls were 27 kilometers long, 3 meters thick and 10 meters high. There were three water cisterns, three moats inside and five towers on which the catapults invented by Archimedes were placed. This extraordinary example of Greek military architecture covered 15,000 sq. meters and walking through the ruins still provides an idea of how imposing it once was. The **Shrine of the Madonna delle Lacrime (of Tears)** is a striking modern building with an enormous reinforced concrete cone seventy-four meters high on top. It can be seen from all parts of the city. It was begun in 1966 and finished in 1994 after the presumed miracle – dating to 1953 – where a plaster statue of the Madonna shed tears, and is a pilgrim site. Inside the image of the young *Madonna* is on the high altar.

Not far from the Shrine, in the **Acradina** district, are the **Catacombs** and the **Church of San Giovanni**. The catacombs were dug into the rock along the walls around the tomb of the first bishop of Syracuse, Saint Marcianus, who was martyred in the third century AD, while the church which was built over the crypt is partially in ruins and has no roof. Rebuilt by the Normans after being destroyed by the Arabs, it still has a fine rose window on the facade and a Byzantine altar inside.

◄ The roofless Church of San Giovanni.

▲ Third-century AD *sarcophagus of Adelphia and Valerius* (Paolo Orsi Museum).

The **Paolo Orsi Archaeological Museum** in **Palazzo Landolina** is one of the most important in Sicily. In its nine thousand square meters it contains eighteen thousand finds, consisting of vases, amphorae, kraters, funerary furnishings, heads (one of *Augustus*), statues of *muses* and *kouroi* and other sculpture (the stone *mother goddess nursing twins* dating to the sixth century BC is particularly charming), while a *sarcophagus of Valerius and Adelphia* dates to the third century AD. Then there is the famous *Landolina or Anadyomene Venus*, a Roman copy of a statue by Praxiteles, so sensuous that Guy de Maupassant " fell in love with her the way one falls in love with a woman ... it is a carnal Venus one dreams of when lying down..."

▲ The *Mother Goddess nursing twins* (Paolo Orsi Museum).

The city has dedicated the **Museum of the Papyrus** to this plant, a symbol of Syracuse. In addition to listing the various species of

▶ *Enthroned Goddess*, sixth-century BC stele, and *Archaic Greek head* (Paolo Orsi Museum).

► The *Anadyomene or Landolina*
(Paolo Orsi Museum).

plants and housing ancient papyrus scrolls (dating to the Pharaohs) it also describes the techniques for making paper throughout the centuries.

Just a few kilometers from Syracuse is the mouth of the small magical **CIANE** River, called *Kianos* or blue by the Greeks because of its clear waters while the banks are covered with dense thickets of papyrus plants up to five meters high, weeping willows and aquatic plants. By boat one can go in an hour to the spring so dear to myth according to which the river was created by the tears shed by Ciane, one of Persephone's nymphs, after her mistress was kidnapped by Pluto and taken to the underworld.

The Ciane River is five kilometers long and empties into the harbor of Syracuse, a meter deep and full of fish of different kinds. The entire area is now a **Nature Reserve**. The first papyrus plants were gifts to Hieron II (265-215) from Ptolemy II of Egypt and since then they have flourished in Syracuse, the only place in Europe. Making paper is an economic resource for the city.

▼ Papyrus plants in the Ciane River Nature Reserve.

Province of Siracusa

■ Avola

Avola is the city of piazzas and almonds. After the earthquake of 1693 it was rebuilt on the plain near the sea by the Jesuit architect Angelo Italia, on a hexagonal plan with the immense *Piazza Umberto I* at the center, from which four streets, forming a cross, move out into four squares. It is the city of almonds because it is surrounded by almond groves, a sacred tree in antiquity, and brought here by the Arabs who founded the city in the ninth century. The almonds, such as the famous *pizzuta*, are exported and used to make the excellent Sicilian sweets or marzipan.

With its thirty thousand inhabitants who make their livelihood from agriculture, Avola has a historical center full of Baroque and Art Nouveau buildings, a fine seafront and an archaeological site with the ruins of a second century BC **Roman Villa** and **Siculi necropoli** scattered over the hills, the *Colles Hyblaei* celebrated by Virgil. Other finds, such as coins, amphorae, sarcophagi, found in the surroundings, are on exhibit in the **Municipal Museum.**

The **Chiesa Madre** of Avola is dedicated to Saint Nicholas of Mira and Saint Sebastian and has a painting by Olivo Sozzi, the *Marriage of the Virgin*, while the lovely Baroque **Church of the Annunciata** has a lavishly decorated concave facade. A votive aedicule is set into the facade of the fine Baroque **Palazzo Guttadauro.**

▼ The charming
Piazza Umberto I in Avola.

■ Noto

What makes the Baroque particularly spectacular in Noto, especially at sunset, is the amber-colored stone. The details, the lavish decoration, the staircases and streets, the pomp and magnificence of the stage set presented by the city bear witness to that marvelous artistic period that blossomed after the earthquake of 1693, making Noto a symbol of a Sicily of marvels.

Named capital of the Baroque by the European Council and a UNESCO World Heritage Site, Noto was rebuilt from scratch in 1703, eight kilometers from Noto antica, on the slopes of the Iblei mountains three kilometers from the sea, by the efficient Sicilian-Spanish Giuseppe Lanza duke of Camastra, backed by the Church but not by the people who wanted to have their city rebuilt on its original site. Palaces, churches, convents and monasteries were created by architects such as Rosario Gagliardi, Vincenzo Sinatra, Domenico Lan-

▲ A steep stepped street in Noto.

dolina, Paolo Labisi, with the skilled local workmen. These buildings line the main street *Corso Vittorio Emanuele* interrupted by three scenic piazzas, *dell'Immacolata, del Mu-*

▼ Baroque balconies of Palazzo Nicolaci Villadorata in Noto.

◄ Church of San Francesco dell'Immacolata.

town planning a *Garden of Stone*. Noto is a silent and austere city despite the fact that there has been a university here since 2003 and it is full of pastry and confectionary shops that reveal the sweet tooth of the Sicilians. The main source of income is tourism, particularly after the collapse in 1996 of the Cathedral dome, which centered world-wide attention on Noto. The nineteenth-century

nicipio and *XVI maggio* in a checkerboard town plan designed by the gifted architect Angelo Italia.
The art historian Cesare Brandi called this masterpiece of architecture and

Porta Reale or **Ferdinandea** marks the entrance to the city on *Via Vittorio Emanuele*. The eighteenth-century architectural complex of the **Church** and **Convent of San Francesco** or **of the Immacolata** preceded by a staircase and with a wealth

▼ The Cathedral of Noto.

▲ ► Palazzo Ducezio,
seat of the Town Hall
and Via Nicolaci during the *Infiorata*.

of Baroque friezes on the portal overlooks *Piazza dell'Immacolata* as does the **Church** and **Monastery of the Salvatore** with thirteen highly decorated windows and facades by Vincenzo Sinatra and Rosario Gagliardi. The **lookout tower** joins the Benedictine monastery to the church. Inside is a **Municipal Museum** with finds from the area and from Eloro. Opposite is the small **Church of Santa Chiara**, built by Rosario Gagliardi on an oval plan and housing a *Madonna and Child* by Antonello Gagini. *Piazza del Municipio* is dominated by the **Cathedral** dedicated to Saints Nicholas and Conrad, a superb example of scenic architecture. Set at the top of a majestic staircase, the Cathedral is flanked by twin bell towers and has a double tier of Corinthian columns and many statues on the facade. Since the Cathedral was built (1693-1780), the domes of the largest church in Noto collapsed four times, the last time in 1996 when the nave gave way.

The **Bishop's Palace** is to the left of the Cathedral while on the right is **Palazzo Landolina**, eighteenth century, built by Vincenzo Sinatra. Right opposite the most important ecclesiastical area, and with a wealth of columns, is the seat of civil power, the Town Hall or **Palazzo Ducezio**, a two-tiered building by Vincenzo Sinatra, with gilded stuccoes and frescoes inside.

In addition to the **Municipal theater**, a late nineteenth-century building, *Piazza XVI Maggio* is known for the **Church** and former **Collegio di San Carlo al Corso** which contains relics of the saint; the eighteenth-century complex of the **Church** and

◄ Church of San Domenico in Noto.

former **Convent of San Domenico**, one of the masterpieces of the Sicilian Baroque by the architect Rosario Gagliardi. A play of darks and lights is created by the convex facade with a portal decorated by friezes. The interior is in red and white marble. The famous street of the prince, *Via Nicolaci*, is one hundred and twenty-two meters of extraordinary beauty, all uphill and scenically ending in the lovely convex facade of the **Church of Montevergini**. Via Nicolaci, with **Palazzo Nicolaci Villadorata** and its fantastic figures supporting the six balconies, is the setting for the *Infiorata* the third week of May in homage to spring in which the entire street is covered by a carpet of flowers.

The **Church of the SS. Crocifisso** overlooking *Piazza Mazzini* in the *Pianazzo* district is dear to the citizens of Noto because inside is the *Holy Thorn* from Christ's crown of thorns, brought from Jerusalem in 1225 by a friar. In the transept is a splendid fifteenth-century *Madonna Bianca* or *of the Snows* by Francesco Laurana.

■ Eloro

The enchanting **archaeological site** of Eloro, founded by the Syracusan Corinthians in the eighth century BC and rediscovered at the end of the nineteenth century by the archaeologist Paolo Orsi, is near No-

▼ The archaeological site of Eloro.

to Marina, on a hill over-looking the sea with a lovely sandy beach and at the mouth of the Tellaro River. Part of the sixth-century BC **fortification walls** and two **gates**, one south and the other north, which led into the city, are still well pre-served. The trapezoidal **Agorà** was to the right of the principal street and still has the remains of dwellings. Excavations have brought to light the vestiges of a small **Temple of Asclepius** of the fourth century BC and the second-century BC **Sanctuary of Demeter** with a portico and Doric columns on the facade and which the Byzantines then transformed into a church. The **Theater** outside the city walls is charming.

◄ Column known as the "Pizzuta" in the northern part of Eloro.

■ Marzamemi

The delightful brightly-colored marine hamlet of Marzamemi, with a fine beach and an almost Caribbean sea, is on the coast, five kilometers from Pachino. Discov-ered in recent years by tourism and the Sicilian upper classes, Marzamemi rose around the tuna fishery and the name, derived from the Greek, means big fishes. Nostalgic for their Afri-ca in that sky full of stars and birds, the Arabs called it *Marsa al hamen*, bay of the doves. The film director Giuseppe Tornatore was seduced by these stars and shot his film *L'uomo delle stelle* (*The Star Maker*) here. It was also the setting for Gabriele Salvatores' film *Sud*. For the past five years the small town has hosted the *International Festival di Frontiera* at the end of July. Marzamemi was a favorite vacation site of the writer Vitaliano Bran-cati, whose red house is on the small islet facing the fishermen's harbor. There are two **Churches**, the old and the new, dedicated to **Saint Francis of Paola**, on the hamlet's only *Piazza*, named *Regina Margherita*.

▼ The small harbor of Marzamemi.

◄ The typical "Pachino" tomatoes.

■ Pachino

A slender stretch of beach, one of the most fascinating and wild in southern Sicily, is on the other side of the natural oasis, the gem of the **Vendicari Reserve**. The way to Pachino, the south-easternmost point of Sicily, is through fresh water marshes, brackish swamps, wooden bridges, rare plants, hosts of birds, the reign of herons and flamingoes, an old tuna fishery with crumbling walls, a fifteenth-century Swabian tower and even an islet lapped by a clear blue sea. Pachino has been called the town with the best climate and more days of sun per year than any other. It is famous for its cherry tomatoes, for the salt flats and is where Vitaliano Brancati (1907-1954) was born. It was founded in the eighteenth century by Prince Starrabana Giardinelli, and has always been inhabited by peoples who came from the Mediterranean, above all Maltese. Traces of Neolithic and Phoenician civilizations, as well as Greek and all the others that passed on the island, are visible in the *Grotte Corruggi* and *Calafarina*. The prince, landowner and founder of the city, designed the eighteenth-century **Chiesa Madre** dedicated to the Holy Crucifix.

▼ Pink flamingoes in the Vendicari Reserve.

▲ The isle of Capo Passero.

▲ The fish market in Portopalo.

■ Portopalo

Portopalo is the southernmost seaside town of Sicily and of Italy, one of the vertexes of the Trinacria, a real window on Africa, where the Ionian and Mediterranean merge. The *Promontorium Pachyni* mentioned by Virgil in the *Aenid* was once joined to Capo Passero island. Recently a third-century BC **necropolis** has been found on the coast.

A popular seaside resort in summer with its clear sea and sandy and rocky coasts, Portopalo has a fascinating variety of African, Maltese and Arabian inhabitants in this charming hamlet with its steep winding streets. A picturesque sight at sunset is the fish auction at the port with cries and colors and a varied humanity. On the islet of **CAPO PASSERO**, thirty-seven hectares of **Nature Reserve** with rare plants, are a **lighthouse** and a seven- teenth-century **coastal tower**. The **ISOLA DELLE CORRENTI** is below the point of the promontory of Portopalo. This small isle is separated from the coast by a kilometer and a half and has a lighthouse as point of reference for sailors, with a splendid bay and an unpolluted sea.

■ Palazzolo Acreide

The haunting remains of the small ancient *Akrai* – place up high – a colony founded in 664 BC by Syracuse, survive at an altitude of eight hundred meters on the Acremente hill between the valleys of the Anapo and Tellaro Rivers. This UNESCO World Heritage Site is forty kilometers from Syracuse.

Greek *Akrai* was rediscovered thanks to Baron Gabriele Judica's passion for archaeology. Excavations have been in course since 1819. Many of the civilizations of Sicily left their mark here. Roman *Acre* was a *civitas stipendiaria* and was destroyed in 827 by the Arabs. It was rebuilt on its original site by the Normans with a defensive *palatium* and the city was thereafter called *Palatiolus* or Palazzolo, a name it kept until the unification of Italy when the municipality gave it the name of Palazzolo Acreide. The earthquake of 1693 destroyed the new city which was then rebuilt in Baroque style, while the millenary stones remained untouched. The aristocratic **Palazzo Judica Caruso**, in the historical center, is known for the length of its balconies, the longest in the world they say, supported by allegorical figures and grotesque masks.

The gem of the archaeological site, which covers barely thirty-five hectares, is the **Theater** in an enchanting setting facing Mount Etna, and defined both by the archaeologist Paolo Orsi and the Greek scholar Ettore Romagnoli as the *Theater of the sky*.

▼ The third-century BC Greek Theater in Palazzolo Acreide.

Dating to the third century BC, the theater had room for only six hundred spectators on 12 tiers subdivided into 9 sectors, while the semicircular **orchestra** is close to the **scena**. A tunnel dug into the rock on the upper part of the cavea led into the **bouleuterion**, where the citizens assembled. Under the theater are the **latomie dell'Intagliata** and **dell'Intagliatella**, from which the Greeks quarried stone for the construction of the monuments, and later used as **hypogea** by the Byzantines and as **catacombs** by the Christians. Other latomie, or quarries, known as **feral temples**, have been brought to light at the foot of

the hill and was where the dead and heroes were venerated.

Twelve bas-reliefs sculptured in the rock have been found near the latomie. These so-called **Santoni** depict the great Mother Cybele, whose cult as *Magna Mater* was of great importance. The base of the **temple of Aphrodite** is still on the old **agorà** while vestiges of the **Roman baths** transformed by the Byzantines into a basilica are nearby.

► The Church of San Paolo.

▼ The carob tree that grows here.

◄ The vast Necropolis of Pantalica.

■ Pantalica

The **Sortino** one sees today is a town that was completely rebuilt in the eighteenth century, with the fine **Chiesa Madre** dedicated to Saint John Evangelist, Baroque, with a wealth of decoration, while the fifteenth-century **Church of Santa Sofia**, restored centuries later and dedicated to the town's patron saint, has a fine portal framed by two tortile columns supporting a bas-relief cornice.

The name Sortino comes from *sciuttini* – those who left – exiles from various historical periods, from neighboring Pantalica which they repopulated. To visit the lovely naturalist and archaeological area of Pantalica, the *city of the dead*, one has to pass through Sortino. Dug into the rock in the great valley through which the Anapo River runs, in the midst of a dense growth of ashes and manna-ashes, carobs and prickly pears, is a honeycomb of 5000 **tombs** and **grottoes** dating to between the thirteenth and eighth century BC. Founded by the Siculi, Pantalica was then Greek and attained its maximum splendor under the Byzantines to which four small villages, refuge of hermits, and three small churches bear witness, while the vestiges of the **Anaktoron**, the king's palace, are all that remain of the old kingdom of *Hybla*.

▼ Ruins of the Anaktoron in Pantalica.

▲ The Plain of Catania with citrus groves and Etna in the background.

■ Lentini

Lentini is the land of the incomparable red oranges, one of the most important agricultural centers of the area of Syracuse, on a hill with terraces covered with orange groves.

Oranges are one of the most important economic resources for this town of over twenty-five thousand inhabitants. Lentini is connected to the sea by two navigable canals and occupies the eastern zone of the fertile *Piana di Catania*, so dear to myth, where the *Laestrygones*, the giants of Etna who ate human flesh, lived and this is why in antiquity it was known as the *Campi Lestrigoni*.

What attracted many was its extraordinary position. In 729 BC the Greeks of Theocles founded *Leontinoi* at the same time as Catania. Subjected by the tyrant of Gela, Hippocrates, in the fifth century BC, it be-

► The Chiesa Madre of Lentini.

came Syracusan despite the Athenian intervention requested by the philosopher Gorgias. The city continued to prosper up to Roman domination and because it had rebelled against Rome it was condemned to be a *città misera*, as described by Cicero. The Arabs subsequently redeemed it and Lentinì continued to grow under the Normans and Swabians, who built a defensive castle, now nothing but ruins. Its decline began when it was destroyed by the two earthquakes of 1540 and 1693. It was rebuilt in the eighteenth century.

To be seen in Lentini is the **Chiesa Madre**, a sober Baroque structure dedicated to Saint Alphius and the brothers Cirinus and Philadelphius martyred in 253 whose mortal remains are in the church in a third-century catacomb. There is also a fine Byzantine silver icon of the *Madonna Odigitria* in the church. Remains of objects from ancient Leontinoi, terra-cotta vases and kraters decorated with *mythological scenes* are in the **Archaeological Museum**.

◄▼ The ruins of the ancient Leontinoi.

The **Archaeological Park** is on the hills of Metapiccola and San Mauro with the remains of the **Porta Syracusana** set against the walls. Traces of dwellings have been found on the **agorà** as well as the ruins of temples and sanctuaries, while tombs of various sizes were found in a **necropolis**. A few huts of the prehistoric village are located on the hill of Metapiccola, identified by historians as *Xouthia*, the city myth says was founded by Xouthos, son of Aeolus.

◾ Augusta

This city, supposedly founded by Augustus in 42 BC, is in a spectacular position, like Syracuse, on an isle on the Ionian sea, between two ports, Megares and Xifoni, joined to the mainland by two bridges.

Rebuilt after the earthquake of 1693, it is now a modern port city of forty thousand inhabitants and has been one of the most important centers of the oil and petrochemical industries of Europe since the 1950s.

Frederick II of Swabia noted both the beauty of the site and its strategic importance and in 1239 he fortified the city and turned it into a military base. Augusta was under Spanish domination from the sixteenth century on, and Spanish culture and customs are still well rooted, and it was provided with numerous forts to combat the Turkish pirates: **Forte Avalos, Vittoria** and **Garcia**. The viceroy Benavides had the **Porta Spagnola** built in 1681.

The historical center of Augusta, Baroque in spirit but with the urban layout given by Frederick, is entered through the Porta Spagnola. The Swabian imperial eagle dominates the facade of the **Town Hall** on *Piazza del Duomo* with the **Chiesa Madre** dedicated to Maria SS. Assunta, while the eighteenth-century **Palazzo Ferreri** is in a Spanish Baroque style.

Frederick's Castle keeps watch seawards. It was built in the thirteenth century to a project by Riccardo da Lentini in a square shape, but only one of the original eight towers still stands. Frequently altered, it was long a prison, and since 2002 the castle has been a venue for cultural events and exhibitions of contemporary art.

▶ The seventeenth-century Porta Spagnola in Augusta.

▲ ▼ The ruins of archaic Megara Hyblaea
and the remains
of the Hellenistic quarters.

■ Megara Hyblaea

The archaeological site of Megara Hyblaea is six kilometers from Augusta, on a low hill facing the sea. For historians it is one of the most important for what it can tell us of an archaic Greek *polis*. Violated by the smoke from the smokestacks of the nearby petrochemical plant and surrounded by industries, the stones of Megara Hyblaea have a long history, beginning with when it was built which according to myth goes back to Daedalus after his escape from the king of Crete. Whatever, the city – says Thucydides – was one of the first Greek colonies in the last decades of the eight century BC on a site already inhabited by indigenous peoples and given to the Greeks by the Siculo king Hyblon, which is why it is called Megara Hyblaea. It soon became rich thanks to trade

▲ The primordial dwellings of Thapsos.

of its pottery and stone utensils throughout the Mediterranean. In the seventh century BC Megara Hyblaea founded the city of Selinunte. Subsequently the democratic Timoleon refounded it in 340 BC after its destruction by the tyrant of Syracuse Gelon, but it was once more razed to the ground by the Romans under the consul Marcellus during the conquest of Syracuse.

The site covers an area of over ten hectares and only a small portion has been explored. Some of the finds are in the **Antiquarium** on site, while others are in the Archaeological Museum of Syracuse, including the lovely stone figurine (archetype of femininity) of the *mother goddess nursing twins*. Parts of the city walls have also been salvaged and a tower gate of the third century BC, while on the sacred area, the **agorà**, the vestiges of a small temple, a shrine and baths have been found in addition to the remains of shops and dwellings. A few sixth and fifth century BC tombs were found in the **necropoli** outside the walls while those of children buried in amphorae and dating to the seventh and sixth century BC were found near the San Cusumano torrent.

■ Thapsos

The archaeological area of Thapsos is near the town of Priolo Gargallo, on the Magnisi peninsula at the center of the gulf of Augusta. It is perhaps the most interesting and singular necropolis of Sicilian protohistory. The archaeologist Paolo Orsi began the excavation campaign, still in course, on the Magnisi peninsula, not much more than a kilometer and a half long and seven hundred meters wide. A **village of primordial dwellings**, dating to between the fifteenth and ninth century BC and known as *Thapsos facies*, was brought to light. The oldest were circular and oval huts, five meters in diameter and with a hearth at the center, and rectangular huts with a courtyard, as well as square huts, and with red pottery vases and amphorae. Grotto tombs were found in the Bronze Age **necropolis**, outside the inhabited center, while other tombs further south, consisted of enormous amphorae without grave goods.

CATANIA

Catania is a volcanic city in all senses, ironic and uninhibited, solar and industrious, proud and tenacious (it rose nine times from eruptions, earthquakes and bombings) and has entrusted its life to Saint Agatha. It is a city open to the seduction and attractions of modernity and is always ready for experimentation. But it is also tied to its ancient history and to the Sicilian culture and soul, populated by gods and nymphs, formed from a melting pot of peoples, races and religions.

Catania is a city of water and fire, stretched out along the lovely Ionian sea and overshadowed by Mount Etna, the volcano upon which the destiny of the city depends, loved and hated, feared and challenged, bearing wealth and destruction. The city is rich, with an active port and industries with the gift of transforming what they touch into money. The city is the first in Sicily with regards to income and it is second in number of inhabitants only to Palermo.

▲ The Feast of Saint Agatha.

▼ View of the city and of Etna.

◄ The scenic courtyard of the *Siculorum Gymnasium*.

de locales are unusual, some with plate-glass walls, such as the *Ciminiere*, a former refinery converted into a culture factory, with two museums, one of the **American Landing** and the other of the **Cinema**. Catania is crowded with tourists (even in winter) and young people who arrive from all over Sicily to attend one of the oldest universities, the **Siculorum Gymnasium** founded in 1434 by Alfonso of Aragon who chose Catania over Palermo.

Crowded with fashionable shops, pubs, restaurants, discotheques, theaters and puppeteers, the avant-garde locales are unusual, some

At night Catania explodes, vibrant with life, with a vocation for entertainment. Something seems to be going on till all hours everywhere

▼ The Vincenzo Bellini Theater.

partying and enjoying good food. The Catanians are devoted to their beloved patron saint, Agatha, martyred in 251 AD because she spurned the proposals of love of the Roman consul Quintianus. Eight churches are dedicated to her and there are processions, illuminations and festivals from February 2 to 5, in which the entire city takes part.

◀▼ Vincenzo Bellini and the gardens dedicated to him.

Catania is a city of culture. Some of the illustrious men who were either born here or chose it as residence include the physicist Ettore Majorana, writers such as Luigi Capuana, Giovanni Verga, Federico De Roberto and Vitaliano Brancati, as well as actors, such as Angelo Musco and Giovanni Grasso. The most famous native son though is the great composer Vincenzo Bellini, affectionately called the "Catanian swan", who wrote such luminous melodic arias. He is celebrated by the city with a **Theater**, a **Museum**, a **Piazza**, a fine **public park**, a monument and even a tasty dish with eggplant: *pasta alla Norma.*

In antiquity it was chosen by the poet Stesichorus and the philosopher Senophanes, while in the seventh century BC the legislator Caronda worked out a code of laws applied by all Greek cities.

The city is a harmony in black and white, with palaces, churches, buildings, rebuilt in black lava stone alternating with white limestone, along the straight long streets that lead to the sea. It was built in a sumptuous flowery Baroque from the ashes of the violent eruption of Etna in 1669 when the lava flow arrived in the city itself, followed not much later by the earthquake of 1693, which brought death and destruction. The men behind eighteenth-century reconstruc-

eroglyphs dedicated to the goddess Isis stands on the elephant's back. At the top is a *statue of Saint Agatha*. On the same square are the former **Collegio dei Chierici** (1694), the **Palazzo degli Elefanti** also Town Hall, the **Porta Uzeda** of 1696 leading to the old port, and the **Cathedral,** dedicated to Saint Agatha. The Cathedral was built in the eighteenth century over the Roman **Achillane baths** by Girolamo Palazzotto, while the lilting two-tiered facade with the statue of the patron saint at the top is by Vaccarini. The interior with its nave and two aisles houses two Aragonese sarcophagi, a Roman one of the

▲▶ The Elephant Fountain, symbol of the city, and the majestic Baroque Cathedral.

tion of Catania were Giuseppe Lanza duke of Camastra, who redesigned the urban layout, and a talented twenty-seven year old abbot-architect Giovan Battista Vaccarini. What little remained of Greek and Roman *Katane* was incorporated into the new buildings.

UNESCO has named Catania a World Heritage Site. Its pulsating heart is in the elegant drawing room of *Piazza del Duomo*, where the streets and districts converge, dominated by the symbol of the city, the **Elephant Fountain** (*o liotru*, as the Sicilians say), made in 1736 by Giovan Battista Vaccarini. An Egyptian obelisk with hi-

third century AD and the tomb of the composer Vincenzo Bellini. The *Tomb of Constance of Aragon* is in the **Chapel of the Madonna**, preceded by an elaborate sixteenth-century *portal* with 14 cameos that narrate the *Life of Mary* while in the right apse is the **Chapel of Saint Agatha**, glittering with gold and stuccoes and with a triptych of *Saint Agatha Crowned by Christ,* a fifteenth-century work by Antonello Ferri. The chapel also contains the rich **Treasury** with the reliquary bust of the saint containing her skull, and her *veil* (tradition says it stopped the flow of lava in 1669) and the precious diamond crown, a gift of Richard the Lionheart to his sister Joan when she married the Norman William II.

Behind the Cathedral, near Porta Uzeda, is the well-known **Palazzo Biscari**, an opulent Baroque with large windows overflowing with allegorical decorations, which was originally designed by Antonio Amato, but took almost a hundred years to finish.

Via Garibaldi, the street opposite the Cathedral, with the **Amenano Fountain,** named after the mythical subterranean river from which it springs and sung by Ovid, is the entrance to the *suq* of the **Pescheria**, the picturesque fish market of Catania, winding through lanes and alleys up to the monumental **Ursino Castle**, seat of the **Municipal Museum** with collections and donations from monasteries and private collectors. The collections include Siciliote and Attic pottery, fragments and heads, such

◄ The terrace of the sumptuous Palazzo Biscari.

as the sixth-century BC *head of an ephebus*. There is also an interesting Picture Gallery or **Pinacoteca**, with a marvelous *Last Judgement* by Fra Angelico.

The Ursino castle, square with cylindrical towers at the four corners, was built between 1239 and 1250 by Riccardo da Lentini for Frederick II as an affirmation of imperial power over the Church.

The long steep **Via Etnea** is the street for promenading, with shops and boutiques and any number of pastry shops (therefore known as the mouth-watering street) that leads up to the slopes of Mount Etna (*a la muntagna*) where rows of jacaranda trees turn stretches purple. Along the street is the **Collegiata** or **Regia Cappella**, considered a marvel of late Baroque, by Angelo Italia and Antonio Amato, with a curvilinear facade by Stefano Ittar. The **Siculorom Gymnasium** with its fine two-tiered court-

yard and two loggias by Vaccarini is on *Piazza dell'Università*, followed by the **gardens of Villa Bellini**, *Piazza Stesicoro* with the *Monument to Bellini* and a few vestiges of a second-century BC **Roman amphitheater** in lava stone. The small **Church of the Carcere (or Prisons)** which incorporates part of the prison where the patron saint of the city, Agatha, was held prisoner, is also of interest.

Via Crociferi, *short, but infinitely beautiful*, to quote Vitaliano Brancati, is the street that ran along the acropolis, the most symbolic and fascinating in Catania, where, as on stage, the Baroque palaces and churches pass in review. After *Piazza San Francesco*, with the church dedicated to the saint, the **Bellini Museum**, and the **Arch of San Benedetto**, come, at the top of a staircase, the **Church** and **Monastery of San Benedetto** (1713

► The picturesque market of the Pescheria.

by Angelo Italia, decorated with stuccoes. Attached piers frame the balconies of the Benedictine monastery, celebrated by Giovanni Verga who set his novel *Storia di una Capinera* here, later made into a film by Franco Zeffirelli. The **Church of San Francesco Borgia** with an austere facade is preceded by two staircases. Opposite is the former **College** and **Church of the Jesuits.** Inside the college, which houses an art school, is a splendid courtyard by Vaccarini, with black and white pebbles. Vaccarini also designed the **Church of San Giuliano,** one of his most interesting Baroque monuments. The church, with a convex facade with a loggia, is topped by a dome. The seventeenth-century unfinished **Church** and **Monastery of San Nicolò** is the largest religious complex in Sicily. The Benedictines

wanted it to be like the churches in Rome.

The **Abbey of Sant'Agata** is on **Via Vittorio Emanuele** that runs parallel to Via Garibaldi. It was built in 1742 by Vaccarini with a sinuous facade and an octagonal dome. Also here are the ruins of the **Roman theater** and of a **Greek Odeon** restructured in the second-third century AD and where theater performances are held in summer.

▼▲ View of the Roman Theater and the Ursino Castle built by Frederick II, seat of the Municipal Museum.

Province of Catania

▲ The imposing Faraglioni (Rocks) of the Cyclops in Aci Trezza.

■ Aci Trezza

After passing **ACI CASTELLO**, a crowded seaside resort at the foot of the Norman **castle** founded in 1076 and now seat of the **Municipal Museum** (marine archaeology), one reaches Aci Trezza. This small town on the sea with a fishing port is a vacation site on the **Riviera dei Ciclopi** or **Faraglioni** (Rocks of the Cyclops) and the **island of Aci** or **Lachea** with eight black basalt rocks rising from the sea, thrown there in his fury, according to Homer, by the blinded Polyphemos against the fleeing Ulysses. There is also a myth that says Polyphemos threw them to kill the shepherd Aci, his rival for the love of Galatea, the beautiful sea nymph. The entire archipelago is a **Marine Reserve**. Aci Trezza has any number

of seafood restaurants and was celebrated in the novel by Giovanni Verga, *I Malavoglia* (*The House by the Medlar Tree*), a classic written at the turn of the eighteenth century.

■ Acireale

Acireale, on a lava terrace dropping sheer to the sea and surrounded by citrus groves, is renowned for its **Terme di Santa Venera** in a park at the entrance to the town. The Greek *xiphonie*, developed by the Romans, were a spa using the beneficial sulfurous waters that gushed from a volcanic spring nearby at a temperature of 22° C. Saint Venera who then became the patron saint was martyred here in the first century AD and the small **Church of Santa Venera al Pozzo** was founded some time in the fourteenth century.

Acireale is also famous for its carnival, with flower-laden allegorical floats, and performances of the Sicilian puppets or *pupi*.

The sixteenth-century **Cathedral**, on *Piazza del Duomo*, is framed by two bell towers with majolica spires.

▲ Puppets, symbols of street theater.

▼ The facade
of the Cathedral of Acireale.

◄ The *Litter of Saint Sebastian*, patron saint of Acireale.

The **Church of San Sebastiano** with a Baroque facade and twelve statues of Biblical figures is perhaps more interesting.

■ Riposto

After passing Giarre, the small seaside hamlet of Riposto merits a pause. The name is derived from *u ripostu*, the cellar, because this is where the wine produced by Giarre and Mascali is preserved. *Rosso di Riposto* is an excellent wine from the hamlet's vineyards and was a favorite with the English.

With a small harbor and the Calabrian coasts across the way, endless rows of citrus trees and an extraordinary garden, the hamlet is unquestionably lovely. The **Kentie Park** is the only one in Sicily with a hundred Kentia or sentry palms (*Howea forsteriana*) over ten meters high which found an ideal habitat here in the early twentieth century.

There is a fine **Chiesa Madre di San Pietro** in Riposto, similar to the Roman church of Saint John Lateran, dedicated to the patron saint. Inside is a precious French *organ*. Only two of the many lookout towers built in Riposto to keep the Turkish pirates at bay are still standing, the **Molo** and the **Managano**.

▼ The Kentie Park in Riposto.

▲ Valle del Bove after the eruption of Mount Etna.

■ Zafferana Etnea

Zafferana Etnea is on the slopes of Mount Etna, on a lava terrace near the **Valle del Bove**. The depressed area (thirty-six square kilometers) was created by the sinking of the top of the crater. The aspect of the valley with lava walls up to a thousand meters high changes with every eruption.

The town, at the mercy of the eruptions, is the point of departure for excursions to the ski fields on Etna. It has been stubbornly rebuilt by the inhabitants after every eruption in which they lose houses, fields and businesses. With its wild beauty the volcano, which they call *a muntagna*, exercises a fatal attraction mixed with deference, halfway between magic and religious.

There is however also a positive side for the countryside is extremely fertile with flourishing citrus groves and hazelnuts.

The *nevaioli*, ice gatherers, used to leave on foot or mule back from Zafferana Etnea to collect ice from the mountain and bring great blocks back to the valley. With the Arab domination, the profession of "ice gatherers" led to the invention of the granita in Sicily. The ice was crushed manually with a special utensil and fruit syrups were added. Once refrigerators were invented the profession of the *nevaiolo* disappeared. The heart of Zafferana Etnea is a terrace-like piazza that overlooks the coast. Next to it is a fine **Chiesa Madre,** pure Baroque in style, dedicated to the Madonna della Provvidenza, patron saint of the town, who is said to have stopped the lava flow more than once, last time in December 1991.

● *L'Etna "a muntagna"*

The mountain rose from the sea 500,000 years ago, is 3,340 meters high, 60 kilometers in diameter and has a perimeter of 212 kilome-

ters. There are 250 erupting cones and 2 craters (the one at the top is an enormous funnel with a circumference of 3 kilometers). Rivers of incandescent lava flow out at a temperature of 1200° C and move at a speed of 15 kilometers. This is Etna, the largest volcano in Europe, one of the most active in the world, relatively young and never still.

The Sicilians call this fascinating volcano *Mongibello* (*Mons Gebel* in Arabic) or *a muntagna*. This mystical mountain dominates the entire coast of eastern Sicily and its snow-capped cone can also be seen from the center of the island. The history of this corner of Sicily is marked by its eruptions, mentioned as early as 475 B.C. by Pindar and Aeschylus. One of the most cataclysmic was the eruption of 1669 that wiped out four towns and left six thousand dead in Cata-

nia. When fear strikes the hearts of the inhabitants, they put their trust, with processions and prayer, in the miraculous intervention of the many saints that people the towns on its slopes: Saint Agatha, Saint Egidio, Saint Anthony and the Madonna. But they know that *a muntagna pigghia, a muntagna dugna* (the mountain takes and the mountain gives), and the flourishing nature, fertile soil, the equivalent of gold for agriculture, are gifts from the mountain. After it has wreaked its fury, everything will be rebuilt. Olive and citrus groves, vineyards, almond and pistachio trees grow on the clods of soft black earth at the base of the volcano while further up the Mediterranean maquis flourishes and still further up there are splendid woods of beech, pine cedars of Lebanon, birch, chestnut and then pastures. At the very top a

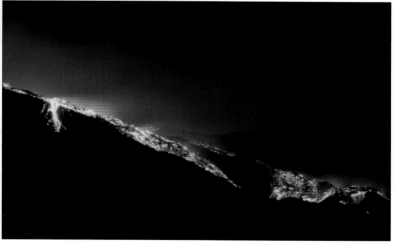

▲ Views of Mount Etna.

two thousand meters one comes to the extraordinary lunar landscape, a stone garden, with reddish sponge-like rocks covered with snow in winter. In spring when the snows melt, what remains is a black desert where life seems impossible and yet cushions of milk vetch grow here, brightly colored meadows of soapwort, the symbol of Etna, and many other native species in unlikely colors. To safeguard the flora and fauna the Sicilian Region has instituted the **Natural Park of Etna**, where fascinating outings can be made and with many shelters where one can rest.

▲ Etna rising up over Randazzo.

■ Randazzo

A charming and solitary medieval town, Randazzo is located on lava rock at seven hundred and sixty meters above sea-level. It is the town closest to the craters of Mount Etna, only fifteen kilometers away, and the Sicilians look on it with awe for it has miraculously always come through unscathed. Randazzo can also be reached by the *circumetnea* train, a hundred and ten kilometers of railroad providing an evocative panorama of the various towns along the slopes of Mount Etna.

The colors of the town are black and green, the black lava stone used in constructing the buildings, churches, houses, farmhouses, dry masonry walls and roads, and the green of the flourishing vegetation and crops that grow so well on this fertile black volcanic soil.

In Randazzo it is either summer, and it is hot for eight months of the year, or winter, which arrives suddenly. Tourism has discovered this tranquil town, a point of departure for excursions on the volcano, and characterized by its air of indolence and a healthy cuisine.

There are eleven thousand inhabitants in Randazzo which was founded by the Byzantines and developed

◄ The lava-stone facade of the Church of Santa Maria in Randazzo.

with the Swabians. Its origins however are much older for ruins dating from the fifth to the second century BC as well as a Greek necropolis have been discovered.

The rooms of the Swabian **Castle** are being restored to house the **Vagliasindi Archaeological Museum**. Up to the sixteenth century the populations spoke three dialects, Lombard, Latin and Greek, and there are three churches which take turns in having services: Santa Maria, San Nicolò and San Martino.

The **Church of Santa Maria** now **Matrice** was the Latin church, built in the thirteenth century. Although it was modified in later centuries it still has its Norman-Swabian architectural layout with tower-like *apses* decorated with arches and small columns. The ornate Gothic *portal* leads into the nave separated from the side aisles by black columns and with sculpture and paintings.

The **Church of San Nicolò dei Greci** also dates to the thirteenth century, later renovated, but still has its *apses* and the *transept*, with a facade in lava stone and white stucco. There is an abundance of sculpture by the Gagini in the nave and side aisles, such as the *Saint Nicholas enthroned* by Antonello Gagini on the altar in the left arm of the transept. The Lombard **Church of San Martino** on the other hand is of Swabian date and was repeatedly renovated. It has a fine fourteenth-century bell tower and an elegant seventeenth-century facade.

■ Bronte

Bronte is known throughout the world for its *green gold*, its excellent pistachios (*frastuca*), grown on 85% of its lava territory, and used in the confectionary industry and in

▼ The famous pistachio groves of Bronte.

▲ The Abbey of Maniace, once owned by Admiral Nelson.

gastronomy. The real specialty of the area is the pistachio *pesto*, but the nuts are also used in cosmetics. The first ten days of October Bronte dedicates a festival, the *sagra del pistacchio*, to this biblical green fruit, picked in alternate years from trees that grow up to five meters high.

Legend says that Bronte, now an agricultural town on the volcano, was founded by the Cyclops Bronte, son of Neptune. The first inhabitants were actually native Siculi, then the Greeks and the other dominations that followed each other in Sicily. The Arabs were the first to organize agriculture and planted pistacchio trees, exporting the nuts throughout the Mediterranean. General Maniace's Byzantines joined the Normans and drove out the Saracens and Bronte acquired a certain prestige with Charles V in 1535 when he united all the neighboring towns. During the Risorgimento Garibaldi sent Nino Bixio to Bronte, who had a few peasants who had rebelled against the landowners shot.

The **Shrine of the Annunziata** in Bronte is one of the most important religious buildings. It dates to the sixteenth century and has a fine *Annunciation* on the high altar, a polychrome marble sculpture by Antonello Gagini. The **Abbey of Maniace** or **Castello di Maniakes** about ten kilometers from the town is worth a visit. It was founded in 1040 on the site where the Byzantine admiral defeated the Arabs, was then donated to the Benedictine monks and then the Basilian religious. In 1799 Ferdinand III gave it, together with the title of duke of Bronte, to the English admiral Horatio Nelson who supported him in repressing the uprisings in Naples. Admiral Nelson never visited either the castle, or Sicily, but his heirs, the Viscounts of Briport, turned it into a luxurious residence and lived here up to 1981 when it became the property of the town. Of interest inside is the small *Chapel of Adelasia* with the painting, brought from Byzantium by General Maniace, of a *Madonna and Child.*

Adrano

Adrano is located to the left of the Simeto River (a few decades ago one could still find amber here) on a lava terrace surrounded by fragrant citrus groves and pistacchio trees. The Greek *Adranon* was founded by Dionysius I in the fifth century BC on the site of a temple dedicated to the indigenous god Adranon, who protected dogs which the priests raised in the shrines convinced that every man was once a dog. The Italian greyhound or Cirneco dell'Etna is still raised here.

▲ The Italian greyhound or Cirneco dell'Etna raised in Adrano.

Many vestiges of the ancient city have been recovered in the frazione of Mendolito, near the characteristic Arab **Bridge of the Saracens**. The vases, amphorae and pytoi, barrels for preserving food, and other objects found in the area are in the **Archaeological Museum of Adrano** in the Norman castle built in the eleventh century by Roger I, who called it *Adernio*.

A large door on the second floor of the castle leads into the *Private Chapel of Adelasia,* the Great Count's wife. Today this agricultural town with thirty-five thousand inhabitants grows oranges, pistachios and produces an excellent honey that is also sent to northern Europe.

Not to be missed is the complex of the **Monastery** and **Church of Santa Lucia**. The church has an elliptical interior, with an abundance of eighteenth-century decorations, a large gilded dome and a delightful rococo choir.

▼ View of Adrano.

■ Caltagirone

Caltagirone is a Baroque city, re-built after the earthquake of 1693. Many of the buildings have been faced with the colored majolica tiles to which the city owes its wealth and history. A **Ceramic Museum,** second only in prestige to the one in Faenza, and an **Art Institute of Ceramics**, are dedicated to this ancient art which the Arabs continued to develop introducing blue and yellow and the glazing technique. The potter's wheel originally came from ancient Crete.

The position is spectacular and the city is in the shape of an amphitheater on the summits of three hills at the foot of the Erei mountains, dominating the plains of Catania and

▲ Majolica pane in the Ceramics Museum

► ▼ The Church of Santa Maria del Monte and panorama of Caltagirone.

Gela. It was a crossroads for the various peoples who passed through, and was inhabited back in Neolithic times. The city which the Arabs called *Qalat-al-Giran* (castle of vases) is divided into two: the lower city seat of civil power and the religious center in the upper city connected by the evocative **staircase of Santa Maria del Monte**. One hundred and forty-two steps, all covered with tiles, are flanked by pottery workshops and for the *Feast of the Patron Saint James* (July 24 and 25) four thousand oil lamps transform them into a brightly colored fantastic display of lights. The **Church of San Giacomo** is also ded-

▲ Staircase of Santa Maria del Monte decorated with small oil-lanterns for the feast of Saint James.

◀ ▼ A characteristic city street and the facade of the Immacolata.

icated to the city's patron saint. It was built in the eleventh century by Count Roger, and contains a splendid sixteenth-century *portal of the Relics* by Domenico Gagini, while the eighteenth-century **Church of the Salvatore** is octagonal in plan and has three apses. Inside is a small *Chapel dedicated to Don Luigi Sturzo*, a priest born in Caltagirone and founder of the Popular Party which then became the Christian Democrat Party.

The thirteenth-century **Church of Santa Maria del Monte** is at the top of the staircase. It was rebuilt after the earthquake. The **Cathedral** which overlooks *Piazza Umberto I* is ded-

icated to Saint Julian and was restructured many times. The facade dates to 1909, the bell-tower to 1954. In the *large park* in the lower city is the small tiled **Theater** and the **Tondo Vecchio**, symbol of the city, an exedra completely faced with majolica tiles. But what everyone photographs in Caltagirone is the **Balaustra Ventimiglia**, a balconied terrace made in the eighteenth century by the great master craftsman Benedetto Ventimiglia. In the Arab quarter the Genoese built the **Church of San Giorgio** in the eleventh century. It was also rebuilt after the earthquake and retains its pointed-arch portal. Of note inside is the fifteenth-century painting of the *Trinity* by the Flemish artist Roger van der Weyden.

◀ The "Tondo Vecchio" faced with majolica tiles.

▲ ► Panorama of Vizzini and the splendid Gothic-Catalan portal of the Chiesa Madre.

Vizzini

Not far from Caltagirone is the medieval hamlet of Vizzini where the writer Giovanni Verga was born in 1840, to which the eighteenth-century **Palazzo Verga** bears witness. Vizzini is a fascinating town that takes the visitor back to a time where progress seems to have been kept at bay and the eight thousand inhabitants continue to live on agriculture, as they have always done, in a plain between two hills. The urban layout is still of Arab imprint, with a labyrinth of small streets and blind alleys that keep out the light. The Normans built a castle and city walls, destroyed in the earthquake of 1693.

The **Chiesa Madre** dedicated to Saint Gregory the Great is in the historical center. It has a splendid Catalan-Gothic portal dating to the fifteenth century. On the altar is a painting by Filippo Paladino of the *Madonna della Mercede*. A fine *Madonna and Child* by Antonello Gagini is in the **Church of the Minori Osservanti**.

MESSINA

Messina lies at the foot of the Peloritani mountains, overlooking the deep blue canal where the Tyrrhenian and Ionian seas meet. Three kilometers separate it from the continent. A bridge is being planned to join it to Italy, as it was five million years ago when a violent earthquake rent the crust of the earth and made Sicily an island. Both economic and political problems have so far barred this initiative, but above all the fact that Messina's territory is subject to earthquakes. Mythically the strait is the home of Charybdis and Scylla, Homer's nymphs changed into monsters who charmed sailors with their songs and then tore them to pieces and dragged them into the abyss. This is how the ancients explained the billows, whirlpools,

tides and currents which are inverted every six hours along the strait and make it so dangerous.

Today it is the **Madonna della Lettera**, at the top of a stele, who welcomes sailors. She is dear to the citizens who placed her above the **Fort of San Salvatore** in memory, says tradition, of the letter the city sent to Our Lady in 42 AD requesting her to support them in adversities.

Every year between May and September swordfish come to the strait to breed and the sea of Messina be-

The "Madonna of the Letter" keeps watch over the deep strait.

comes the theater of a *mattanza*, or killing spree, with the fishermen on board the feluccas harpooning and capturing the big fish, filling the air with their cries and litanies.

Messina is a port city, with a natural sickle-shaped inlet, protected by the San Ranieri peninsula. One of the city's major sources of wealth, now as in the past, are the activities connected with its port.

The colonists who founded it in the eighth century BC called it *Zancle*, because of the sickle shape of its harbor. This is where Antonello da Messina (1430-1479), that brilliant master of the portrait and precursor of the realism that culminated two centuries later with Caravaggio, was born. Today it is a vital, busy modern city, with broad streets and an elegant shorefront boulevard, piazzas and new buildings in reinforced concrete. Little is left of old Messina, with its history of epidemics of cholera and plague and the earthquakes that

▼ ► The Cathedral of Messina with its tall bell tower and view of the nave.

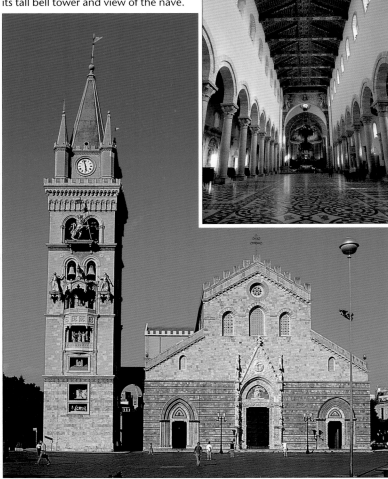

◄ The Orion Fountain.

thedral has a complicated mechanical astronomical clock made in 1930 in Strasbourg by the Ungeren brothers and which still works.

The only original piece inside is a sixteenth-century statue of *Saint John the Baptist* by Antonello Gagini. The others are all copies. The **Cathedral Treasury** contains a priceless veil of 1668, the *Golden Mantle*, embroidered with precious stones and used for Orthodox services.

The **Orion Fountain** by Giovanni Angelo Montorsoli across from the cathedral dates to the sixteenth century and is decorated with statues that symbolize the Tiber, Nile, Camaro and Ebro Rivers. Nearby is the fine **Church of Sant'Annunziata dei Catalani**, a twelfth-century Arab-Norman jewel. The barrel-vaulted nave is separated from the cross-vaulted side aisles by ogee arches.

razed it to the ground. The last one in 1908 left eighty thousand of a total of one hundred and sixty thousand inhabitants dead. And then in World War II the city was bombed. After every catastrophe the city tenaciously rebuilt and began its life anew, although there were no architects as in other cities who created masterpieces from the rubble.

Heart of the city is *Piazza del Duomo*, with the **Cathedral** dedicated to the Virgin of the Assumption, built in 1150 by the Normans and rebuilt after the various earthquakes. It still has three Gothic portals, the one in the center decorated with putti, columns, statues of saints and kings. The bell-tower next to the ca-

► View of the apses of the Santissima Annunziata dei Catalani.

Opposite the church is the *Monument to John of Austria* who defeated the Turks in the Battle of Lepanto in 1571.

The **Church of Santa Maria degli Alemanni**, the two side aisles separated from the nave by columns with original capitals, is Gothic.

In addition to fragments, archaeological finds, Greek and Roman statues and Byzantine mosaics, the **Regional Museum** has a splendid **Pinacoteca** with masterpieces such as the *Polyptych of Saint Gregory*, five oil panels, and the small painting of a *Madonna and Child*, by Antonello da Messina, the *Resurrection of Lazarus* and the *Adoration of the Shepherds* by Caravaggio, a fourteenth-century statue, the *Madonna of the Lame (degli Storpi)* by the Sienese

◄▲ Details of the *Polyptych of Saint Gregory*, by Antonello da Messina (Regional Museum).

Goro di Gregorio, a *Supper at Emmaus* and the *Incredulity of Saint Thomas* by Alonso Rodriguez, a painter from Messina who was a pupil of Antonello da Messina, and a sixteenth-century statue of the *Madonna dell'Itria* by Alessandro Allori.

There are also delightful sites for outings, popular both with the locals and tourists, with a crystal clear sea, rocks and extraordinary green landscapes: **Torre Faro** with tall

▲ *Resurrection of Lazarus*, by Caravaggio (Regional Museum).

rocks rising sheer from a clean transparent sea, the two small lakes, *Pantano Grande* and *Pantano Piccolo* of **GANZIRRI** with groundwater, a small fishing village where shellfish, above all oysters, are grown, and a sixteenth-century **tower** that overlooks it all. The **beaches of Mortelle** have fine white sand with one small beach after the other bathed by a sea where the waters of the Tyrrhenian and the Ionian mingle.

► The beach of Sant'Alessio on the coast of Messina.

Province of Messina

■ Taormina

Taormina, perched on a terrace two hundred meters from the sea on the Tauro promontory in sight of Calabria and Etna, has always been the aristocratic paradise of elite tourism, called the *island in the sky*.

Taormina is characterized by its light, silence, fragrance of lemons, bougainvillea that spill over every corner, lanes, palaces and churches, nature, sea and beaches. It is a conglomeration of art and history and is what seduced the travelers of the Grand Tour, such as Goethe, writers and intellectuals, film directors and actors, such as Liz Taylor and Richard Burton who fell in love here, and the many VIPs who return every summer. The mild climate is a drawing card and Taormina has everything one needs in the way of high society and recreation, for the body and the spirit, and events and reviews of *Haute Couture*, *Cinema* and *Art Festivals* that are always packed are organized in its architectural gems.

There is a cable car to take visitors down to the sea, to one of the surrounding bays and inlets, with beaches of sand, rocks and pebbles such as Capo Taormina, Mazzarò la mon-

▼ View of the splendid Isolabella and of Capo Sant'Andrea.

dana where the VIPs go; Isolabella and Capo Sant'Andrea. The **Bay of Isolabella**, the most photographed (it is also a WWF Reserve), is a green islet with a castle and a slender sandbar that connects it to the mainland. **Capo Sant'Andrea** is a blue grotto in the midst of the fragrant Mediterranean macchia.

Teokles, the Chalcidian sailor who was shipwrecked on these coasts (or pirate some say), realized that these places were kissed by fate and a benign nature and in the eighth century BC he founded *Tplauroménion*. It was later occupied in 358 BC by the Syracusan tyrant Dionysius I who destroyed the city. Subsequently Andromachus repopulated it with people from Naxos. After the Roman domination, it took the Arabs a century to conquer it and in 962 it was

▲ Corso Umberto I,
the street of the promenade.

razed and in revenge Ibrahim Ibn Ahmed brutally killed the bishop Procopius. His successors were less brutal and loved the town and left monuments that can still be seen such as the cubic **Al Kabah** tower of the Corvaja palace, buildings and water cisterns. The Normans called it *Almoezia* and drove out the Arabs and reinstated Christianity, building churches and convents.

In Taormina *lu passiu*, the promenade, moves along *Corso Umberto* I – the old Roman *Via Valeria* that joined Messina to Catania – in the midst of fashion boutiques, antique shops and historical bookstores, elegant hotels, chocolate and pastry shops with cherry wainscoting. Nearby is *Via Teatro Greco*, with the extraordinary and famous **Theater**, the personification of Taormina. In 1787 when Goethe saw it he was overcome by its beauty and magic, in perfect symbiosis with the landscape.

The theater which the Greeks built in the third century AD and which was then modified by the Romans

▲▼ Bird's-eye view of Taormina and the enchanting third-century BC Greek Theater.

for their gladiator games is second in size to that of Syracuse. The **Cavea** measures 109 meters and is encircled by a double vaulted **colonnade**. There was room for up to five thousand spectators in the tiers, while the **scena** opened off the **orchestra**. To the right of the cavea are the remains of a small **Temple** and an **Antiquarium** contains the vestiges found. The **Naumachie**, a hydraulic system decorated with niches and built by the Romans to collect rain water, are in *Piazza Vittorio Emanuele*, in the area of the ancient Roman Forum. Vestiges of an **Odeon** of Imperial age

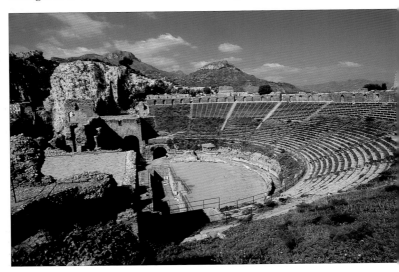

◄ The Naumachia, a retaining structure of the imperial age.

ing in the **Clock Tower** and the **Porta di Mezzo**, after which comes the hamlet of Taormina and the austere Cathedral.

The **Cathedral** is dedicated to Saint Nicholas and was built in the thirteenth century. Renovated in the fifteenth and eighteenth century, it still has the Norman architectural layout. The facade has a rose

were incorporated in 1600 in the **Church of Santa Caterina**, and then there are the **Baths** and **Palazzo Corvaja**, which hosted the Sicilian Parliament in 1410. Built in the fifteenth century, it incorporates Arab and Norman structures and has merlons, inlays of lava stone and a splendid Gothic portal. Inside is the **Museum of Folk Art and Traditions**.

The **Churches of Sant'Agostino** and **of San Giuseppe**, with Baroque staircases, overlook the charming panoramic terrace of *Piazza IX Aprile* end-

▼ ► The Church of Sant'Agostino in Piazza IX Aprile and the Clock Tower.

▲ The splendid setting of the scena in the Theater.

▲ ► The austere thirteenth-century
Cathedral of San Nicolò
and the Palace
of the Dukes of Santo Stefano.

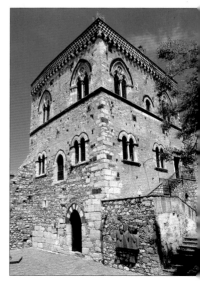

window and two monofores while
inside, a nave with two side aisles,
are a *Madonna and Child* by Antonello de Saliba and a fifteenth-century *Visitation* by Antonino Giuffrè.
The **Palace of the Dukes of Santo
Stefano** is an example of Chiara-
montana architecture in a square
form and with bifores. In style it is
similar to the **Badia Vecchia** or **Ba-
diazza**, a Norman building remodeled in the thirteenth century.

▲ The splendid panorama of Taormina from Castelmola.

Castelmola

Above Taormina, after five kilometers of winding road, is Castelmola, a picturesque medieval locality falling sheer to the sea, lovely and seductive, with dizzying panoramas like those of Taormina but without the worldliness and clangor. It was a favorite with those who wanted a place to relax, nobles and financiers. Winston Churchill and Lord Mountbatten came here and people still recount the risqué adventure of a local peasant with the lovely Frieda, D.H. Lawrence's wife, during the three years they stayed in nearby Taormina. After conquering Taormina, Dionysius I set his acropolis on what had been the **fort** and the Arabs later built a defensive **fortress** there, now only ruins. Nearby is a **Shrine of the Madonna della Roccia** and the remains of an archaic **necropolis** with grotto tombs.

Castelmola is a pretty hamlet of a thousand souls, with flowering balconies, a few narrow streets with black and white mosaic paving. *Porta Saraceni* is the entrance to the town and there is a panoramic terrace, *Piazza Sant'Antonio*. The **Parish Church** dedicated to San Nicola is on the small *Piazza del Duomo*. There are a few souvenir shops and many selling embroideries and old lace, as well as bars with the local specialties such as dry almond cookies, *piparelli*, and a sweet almond wine.

Giardini Naxos

Giardini Naxos is a popular seaside resort on the Ionian coast in the bay that stretches from *Capo Schisò* to *Capo Taormina* with pointed lava rocks, a fine beach and a splendid deep blue sea that fascinated the French film director Luc Besson who shot his film *Le Grand Bleu (The Big Blue)* here in 1988.

The archaeological site of the glorious ancient Naxos, founded according to the historian Thucydides in 734-

▲ The bay of Mazzarò.

733 BC by *Tukles* (Teocles), a Chalcidian from *Kalkis* (Euboea), joined by the *Nassi*, is in Giardini Naxos. It was the first of the Greek colonies in Sicily which shaped the history of the entire island, autonomous from and eventually rivals of the mother country. Three centuries later Naxos was destroyed by the Syracusans of Dionysius I because it had allied itself with Athens.

The ruins in this important **archaeological area** testify to various epochs: from the archaic, the eighth century BC that cover around ten hectares, to that of the seventh century BC, up to the fifth-fourth century BC. Sixth-century BC fortification **walls** have been recovered as have the remains of dwellings, terra-cotta kilns, traces of orthogonal roads.

In Capo Schisò, the ancient *sacred area of Santa Venera*, the vestiges of the city gates, the large shrine and a temple dedicated to Aphrodite (sixth-fifth century BC) have been brought

▲ Terra-cotta kilns in ancient Naxos.

▲ The crowded beach of Giardini Naxos.

to light. There is an **Archaeological Museum** at Capo Schisò with Greek finds such as mask antefixes, statuettes of gods and an *enthroned god-* *dess,* as well as vases and kraters, a *bronze parade helmet* and objects from earlier civilizations present in Naxos as far back as Neolithic times.

■ Gole dell'Alcantara

Upon leaving Giardini Naxos an excursion to the fascinating surreal Gole dell'Alcantara is a must. Up above is the town of **FRANCAVILLA DI SICILIA**, founded by the survivors of Naxos, and then the Norman fort of Ruggero di Lauria with the remains of the *Castrum Leonis*.

The Gole dell'Alcantara, now the **River Park of Alcantara**, are spectacular deep gorges in the rock created by the eruption of a secondary crater that created rock walls and cavities in extravagant shapes, along which runs the Alcantara River fed by a spring in the Nebrodi mountains. Wearing rubber boots, one can go up river for a hundred and fifty meters in a particularly beautiful setting with the sun occasionally coming through, and populated by the frogs the Arabs loved. Crocodiles where also raised in *al Quantarah* brought to Sicily by the Arabs together with the pistachio trees.

■ Milazzo

The thirty thousand inhabitants of Milazzo, a city on the Tyrrhenian coast, make their living from seaside tourism, agriculture, industry with a port for trade and point of departure for the Aeolian Islands. In the Middle Ages Milazzo developed in three zones: the **walled city**, the **hamlet**, and the **lower city**. Alive and exuberant, with lovely beaches, palms along the esplanade and a sandbar on the sea, **CAPO MILAZZO** has look out towers, rich villas and a lighthouse with a panoramic terrace overlooking the rocks at its base from which the sea, the Aeolian Islands and Calabria can be seen. A staircase leads to the small **Shrine of Saint Anthony of Padua**, full of ex-votos. Tradition says that in 122 a storm forced the saint to land here. Nearby i the **cave of Polyphemos** where Ulysses is said to have encountered Polyphemos.

Milazzo was the Greek *My*

◄ The spectacular Gole dell'Alcantara.

▲► The imposing Castle of Milazzo,
built by Frederick II,
and the Basilica
of San Francesco di Paola.

lai, founded by the Greeks of Zancle (Messina) in the eighth century BC. After its occupation by the Syracusans it became Roman. In 260 BC the Carthaginian fleet was defeated in these waters by the Romans under the consul Caius Duilius. Many centuries later, in 1860, Giuseppe Garibaldi defeated the Bourbon army here.

A fourteenth-century BC **necropolis** with *pytoi* and tombs containing skeletons in a fetal position and grave furnishings from the Thapsos culture has been found.

A pleasant walk is through the historical center of Milazzo with its narrow streets, corridors, courtyards and lanes, and with scenic Baroque palaces next to humble dwellings.

In the **old city**, surrounded by a first circle of fifteenth-century walls, is the **Castle** built between 1237 and 1240 by Frederick II. This imposing structure with its five towers was subsequently strengthened by Alfonso of Aragon. Of interest inside is the **Hall of Parliament**. Not far off, in-

side another circle of walls, is the **old Cathedral**, seventeenth-century Baroque in style but in a state of disrepair, and now closed to the public. In the **hamlet**, surrounded by the third circle of walls, are the **Church** and **Convent of the Rosario**, the old headquarters of the Inquisition, and the Baroque **Basilica of San Francesco di Paola**, on a double ramp of stairs.

In the **lower city**, near the sea, is the fifteenth-century **Church of San Giacomo** with paintings by Antonello de Saliba.

■ Tindari

The pearl of the Tyrrhenian, Tindari, stands on a rocky headland overlooking the sea in sight of the Aeolian Islands. At its base a sandy beach embraces three tiny lakes, Verde, Marinello and Mergolo, which magically change as the currents and tides create new multiform tongues of sand. Salvatore Quasimodo was charmed by the magic of Tindari and wrote a lovely poem to the city.

The **Shrine of the Black Madonna** contains a statue of the *Black Madonna* that arrived mysteriously from the East and is thought to be miraculous. The Shrine is located on the old acropolis and keeps watch over Tindari with a never-ending flow of pilgrims coming to pay their respects. The structure there now is recent and has incorporated the old sixteenth-century shrine.

Aside from the legend that affirms that Tindari was founded by the *Tyndaridae* or *Dioscuri*, sons of Tyndareus king of Sparta, father of the beautiful Helen for whom the Trojan war was fought, *Tyndaris* was one of the last Greek colonies in Sicily, founded by Dionysius I of Syracuse in 396 BC and partially sunk into the sea when, as Pliny tells us, a seaquake struck in the first century AD.

▼ The romantic tiny lakes of Marinello.

The white Greek **Theater** facing the sea is a late fourth-century BC structure (diameter 63 meters with 28 tiers divided into 11 sectors) adapted by the Romans for their games. Of the ancient third-century BC **walls** only those on the south, with a tower and a gate are still extant. Traces of shops, dwellings, a few columns and buildings such as the third-century BC

▼ The splendid white Greek Theater of Tindari overlooking the sea and the ruins of a Roman dwelling.

baths with mosaic floors remain of the terraced **insula**. The mosaic in the *frigidarium* depicting athletic contests is well preserved, while one of Dionysius with a panther is signed by the slave of the Syracusan tyrant Agathon.

Only the ground floor are remains of the **Roman Basilica** or **Gymnasium** with barrel vaulting. Finds from the excavations and a colossal stone *head of the emperor Augustus* are in the five rooms of the **Archaeological Museum**.

◼ Patti

Following the lovely *costa delle ginestre* on the promontory of Capo Calavà, falling sheer to the sea – where the ruins of the fourteenth-century town of **Gioiosa Vecchia** are also to be found – one arrives at **MARINA DI PATTI**, a stupendous seaside resort on the gulf of the same name, with the vestiges of a **Roman villa** destroyed by the fourth-century AD earthquake in an area of twenty thousand square meters. The villa, still being excavated, was discovered by chance in 1976 during the building of the Palermo-Messina highway. So far part of the *peristyle*, a few polychrome floor mosaics, a *room with three apses*, and a portion of the *baths* have come to light.

The town of Patti is further inland. In 1094 Roger of Altavilla built a large abbey here, which was burned by Frederick II of Aragon to punish the Benedictine monks who had remained faithful to the Angevins. Centuries later the city was repeatedly sacked and burned by the terrible pirate *Khair ad din* also known as Ariadeno Barbarossa or Redbeard.

The lovely **Cathedral** of Patti is dedicated to Saint Bartholomew and is an eighteenth-century renovation of a preceding Norman church founded by Roger II for the mortal remains of the queen mother Adelasia. Widow of the great Count Roger, she died in 1118 in a convent in Patti, the exile chosen after her marriage with the king of Jerusalem, Baldwin, fell through. In addition to her sarcophagus, the church has a **Treasury** with precious objects including gold-work, a fourteenth-century chalice, and antique texts.

◄ The Tomb of the Countess Adelasia in Patti.

► Lucio Piccolo baron of Calanovella, poet and bard of Sicily.

Capo d'Orlando

Capo d'Orlando lies on the Tyrrhenian coast at the base of the Rocca del Semaforo with its citrus groves, and the promontory of Capo d'Orlando rising up above. This pleasant seaside resort faces onto the rocks that rise from the sea and is particularly popular in summer with its beaches and **coasts**, such as that of the **Saraceni**, high and ragged. It was already inhabited in the first millennium BC and Greeks, Romans, Byzantines and Arabs competed with each other for this strategically placed town. Tradition says that when Charlemagne visited it, he was so delighted by the beauty of the place that he decided to call it after his champion (paladin) Orlando. Facing the sea, a few kilometers from the city center, is a splendid villa now **Museum**. Until he died in 1969 it was home to the poet Lucio Piccolo baron of Calanovella, cousin of Giuseppe Tomasi di Lampedusa, discovered by Eugenio Montale when the *Canti*, a choice selection of poems that reveals the Sicilian soul, was published. On the promontory, with a panorama that reaches as far as the Aeolian islands, are the **Shrine of Maria Santissima** of 1598 and the ruins of the fourteenth-century **Castle**.

▼ Panorama of Capo d'Orlando.

▲ A stretch of Costa San Gregorio.

In the outskirts, at San Gregorio in contrada Bagnoli, the remains of the **baths** of a Roman villa have been found, the *frigidarium* with three rooms, the *tepidarium* and the *calidarium*.

■ Halaesa

Continuing along the Tyrrhenian coast, three kilometers from the pleasant town of Castel di Tusa, is the ancient *Alèsa Arconidea*, on a hill surrounded by olive trees. This Greek colony was founded in 403 BC by the tyrant Archonides II, ruler of Herbita. In 263 BC during the Punic War, it became a *free* and *autonomous* city after allying itself with Rome. It prospered with trade and coined its own

▼ The ruins of a Roman Temple in Halaesa.

money. Decline set in when it was governed by two magistrates under the emperor Augustus and subsequently was the object of extortion by the praetor Gaius Verrus.

Excavations of the ancient Greek colony (still in course) have brought to light stretches of **walls**, the remains of a **theater**, the stylobate of a temple and the **agorà**, the columns of a portico and a grid town plan, while the necropolis lies outside the walls.

■ Eolie, isole (Aeolian Islands)

Seven volcanic cones offshore Milazzo form the Aeolian archipelago, dream islands surrounded by a crystal-clear sea. Alicudi, Filicudi, Lipari, Panarea, Salina, Stromboli and Vulcano are where tourists go to get the best of what Sicily has to offer: sun, sea, a good climate, magical landscapes, flourishing vegetation, spa waters, swimming in water with a wealth of aquatic flora including red gorgonians, meadows of poseidonia oceanica and starfish, an excellent cuisine, entertainment, relaxation and silence. These islands are volcanic outcrops that emerged from the sea a million years ago. Two of them, Vulcano and Stromboli, are still active. Recently another underwater volcano has been discovered two kilometers from the latter, at a depth of five hundred meters. Fertile and with birds of all kinds as well as playful dolphins, they have been declared a World Heritage Site by UNESCO.

VULCANO, named by the Romans in honor of the god Vulcan, smells of sulfur. The smallest of the four small volcanoes that make up the island is Vulcanello and the largest and most active is Vulcano della Fossa. It is known for the therapeutic properties of its sulfurous mud and fumaroles or jets of steam and sulfur vapors rising from the clefts in the *faraglioni di Levante*. There is a haunting beauty to the island with its sulfur yellow and alum white rocks. The beaches include the *Spiaggia del-*

▼ Spectacular view of rocks and craters colored yellow by sulfur at Vulcano.

▲ The square white houses typical of Stromboli.

l'Acqua Calda, with hot water throughout the year, that of *Ponente* or of the black sands with cane brakes (the women use the canes for making baskets and the men for their fishpots), and the semi-deserted *Gelso* with its lighthouse, all within walking distance.

STROMBOLI. After seventeen years of lull, in 2002 this volcano began erupting, resulting in a seaquake when two landslides took place in the wake of the fiery volcanic lava flow. The volcano is an important drawing card for the many tourists who climb up four hundred meters to enjoy the spectacle. It is also fascinating at night from the sea when the volcanoes shoot incandescent stones high into the sky. The Romans thought of it as the lighthouse of the Mediterranean. **Ginostra** and **Stromboli**, **San Vincenzo** and **Ficogrande** are the hamlets on the island of Stromboli, a few square white houses nestled in a flourishing vegetation of olives, vines, with bougainvillea on the walls. The population numbers fewer than a thousand, and donkeys are used for transportation. Stromboli, the island favored by intellectuals and thinkers, in 1949 witnessed the love story between Roberto Rossellini and Ingrid Bergman during the shooting of the film "*Stromboli*".

◄ The hamlet of Salina.

► The lava beach of Pollara at Salina.

SALINA, the old Greek *Didyme*, second largest in the archipelago, is the greenest of the Aeolian islands with vines, capers, fragrant broom. Salina (named after the old salt-pans at the small town of Lingua) is dominated by two inactive volcanic cones and is in vogue for those who want beauty without noise and confusion. The lovely Mount Fossa delle Felci and the splendid amphitheater-shaped lava beach of *Pollara* provide unforgettable sunsets. The beach became famous with Massimo Troisi's last film "*Il Postino*" with Maria Grazia Cucinotta. The cuisine of Salina offers any number of dishes based on capers, grown here since antiquity. When they blossom the fragrance of these white evanescent caper flowers inundate the island. One in particular of the excellent local wines, Malvasia, a muscatel, is the best in Sicily.

PANAREA is barely three square kilometers in size, the smallest of the islands, but the bluffs are exclusive and fashionable, the center of night life and riotous fun. The six surrounding cliffs can be reached on the small double ended fishing boats in the small harbor. Many Italians from the north have bought splendid white houses in the island's three districts:

▼ The small and exclusive island of Panarea.

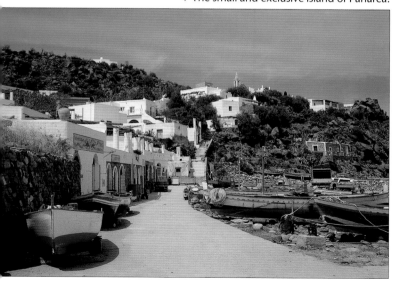

◄▲ The silent Alicudi and the prehistoric village of Capo Graziano in Filicudi.

Ditella, **San Pietro** and **Drauto** (after the pirate Dragut). At the charming **Capo Milazzese** the ruins of the prehistoric village overlook the splendid bay of *Cala Junco* between two cliffs and the emerald sea. *Spiaggia Fumarola* is an isolated place with a pebbly beach where one can go swimming in absolute peace accompanied by the cries of the seagulls.

ALICUDI is covered with purple heather and prickly pear. It is the island of silence, mysterious and distant, without roads, only mule paths and donkeys. The few vacation houses are those the fishermen make available for those who want a vacation of sun and sea.

FILICUDI like Alicudi is wild, full of volcanic craters. The rocky coasts rise sheer from the sea but in some stretches, such as **Capo Graziano**, they are a bit friendlier. A *prehistoric village*, older than the one in Panarea, has been discovered here. The

pebbly beach *Pecorini a Mare* is right below the village. The *Grotta del Bue* is a cavern colored yellow, pink, green and azure, due to the volcanic gases. **LIPARI**, the largest and most densely

► The Spanish Castle of Lipari.

populated of the Aeolian Isles, is a black and white island: white with pumice and black with obsidian. It has tourist facilities and five small towns: **Canneto**, **Acquacalda**, **Quattropani**, **Piano Conte** and **Lipari**.

The principal town is Lipari, with splendid square houses colored pink, yellow, green, Pompeiian red, crowded together. There are cafes, hotels and restaurants.

Lipari is the island which appeared to Homer's Ulysses as an enchanted land. **Monte Pilato** with its white pumice and **Rocche Rosse** black with obsidian are magical, dropping sheer to the sea, with spectacular color contrasts. The most famous beach, with a white pumice sand, is

◄ Theater masks in the Aeolian Archaeological Museum.

in the town of **Canneto**. The panorama of the island, the sea, the *faraglioni* and Vulcano from the *lookout point of Quattrocchi* is spectacular.

The interesting **Museo Archeologico Eoliano** (Aeolian Archaeological Museum) in the Spanish castle has prehistoric finds, sculptured obsidian and marine archaeology, a section dedicated to volcanology, and a reconstruction of the Bronze Age necropolis as well as amphoras, vases, and the famous theater masks.

Distributor for Sicily:
PROMOLIBRI
di Luigi Zangara & C. S.a.s.
Via Aquileia, 84
90144 Palermo
Tel. +39-091.6702413
Fax +39-091.6703633

Publishing editor: Barbara Bonechi
*Text revision, coordination, iconographic
research:* Lorena Lazzari
Cover, layout and graphic design:
Paola Rufino, Sabrina Menicacci
Photographs:
Melo Minnella (Palermo);
Luigi Nifosì (Scicli) www.luiginifosi.it;
Fotostudio Piero Orlandi
(Lainate - Milan);
Massimo Listri (Florence);
Carfagna & Associati (Rome);
Theater director
Beppe Ghiglioni (Florence);
Bonechi Archive - Edizioni
"Il Turismo" S.r.l.
The plan of Sicily was kindly granted by:
Edizioni Multigraphic S.r.l. - Florence -
www.edizionimultigraphic.it
English Translation: Studio Comunicare
Photolithography:
Puntoeacapo S.r.l., Florence
Printed by: Liongraf S.r.l., Florence

ISBN: 88-7204-606-8

*Particular thanks
to the Diocesan Museum of Palermo
for granting use of the photos
and for their invaluable collaboration.*

• *The location of the artworks
in this book corresponds to their
whereabouts as the book goes to print.*
• *Everything possi ble has been done
to ascertain the legitimate owners
of the rights for individual illustrations.
In case there have been
any involuntary omissions,
we will be happy to pay the use fees.*

TABLE OF CONTENTS